In A Clear Concise Arabic Tongue

A collection of short plays by
Yussef El Guindi

BROADWAY PLAY PUBLISHING INC
New York
www.broadwayplaypublishing.com
info@broadwayplaypublishing.com

In A Clear Concise Arabic Tongue
© Copyright 2021 Yussef El Guindi

All rights reserved. This work is fully protected under the copyright laws of the United States of America. No part of this publication may be photocopied, reproduced, stored in a retrieval system, or transmitted, in any form or by any means, electronic, mechanical, recording, or otherwise, without the prior permission of the publisher. Additional copies of this play are available from the publisher.

Written permission is required for live performance of any sort. This includes readings, cuttings, scenes, and excerpts. For amateur and stock performances, please contact Broadway Play Publishing Inc. For all other rights please contact Samara Harris Anderson, Michael Moore Agency, samara@michaelmooreagency.com.

Cover art by Andrew Skwish

First edition: December 2021
I S B N: 978-0-88145-916-6

Book design: Marie Donovan
Page make-up: Adobe InDesign
Typeface: Palatino

CONTENTS

Dedication iv
Author's note v
Further notes & acknowledgments xi
BRASS KNUCKLES 1
PICKING UP THE SCENT 13
THE TYRANT 33
THE BIRDS FLEW IN 53
THE MONOLOGIST SUFFERS HER MONOLOGUE 65
SO UNLIKE ME 75
THE SNIPER 91
A MARRIAGE PROPOSAL 107
THE REVIEW 141
RADICAL DEPARTURE 157

DEDICATION

Once again, and long overdue, to Robin Rockey

AUTHOR'S NOTE

Imagine a dystopia where you, a theater practitioner, someone who loves theater, never see yourself represented on any stage anywhere. You do see monstrous distortions of yourself in Hollywood and Western movies that makes you sink in your seat—in shame, embarrassment—and later, when remembering, go into little fugue states of rage, because rage usually happens when you feel powerless and don't know how to respond to a relentless, dehumanizing venom unspooled at 24 frames per second.

In theater-land, on the other hand, there is *no* representation. Nobody of your ilk is present to be *mis*represented. No Arabs, Muslims, or Middle Eastern people occupy any part of the stage you're drawn to. In this profession that purports to be a truth teller, a reflection of the world we live in, you are not seen, heard or acknowledged in any way. (I'm sure someone might point to some appearance in the pre-2000s, but that would fall under the category of few-and-far between and too inconsequential to create any kind of cultural impact.)

But here's the thing: after years of ingesting this venom and void, this state of cultural invisibility wasn't even felt as a condition because there was no expectation *for* visibility. Even for someone as sensitive to representation as I was, I didn't truly believe my stories belonged up there on the big stages. That was where the angst and humor, the drama and comic foibles of a certain demographic played out. Not my demographic. Why would my demographic belong up there on those LORT stages? Such is the all enveloping cultural aesthetics of this dystopia that even I believed that my stories of Arabs/ Muslims/ Middle Easterners only belonged (if they were to exist at all) way out in the fringiest of fringe theaters.

This lack of expectation on my part couldn't even be considered as some kind of self-abnegation or loathing. There was no assembled self to loathe. A communal self is created in the stories a community shares with each other, about each other, and since I saw no representation of myself anywhere in my profession, I hadn't yet, in a cultural sense, been created.

In this dystopia I had become a well-conditioned, good little theater practitioner who didn't know he could complain about this state of affairs. I didn't know I could push back and address the gate-keepers of theater with their deep indifference, even antipathy, to all things Arab, Muslim and Middle Eastern. And if I had had the wherewithal to speak up back then, I knew they could ignore me with no consequences. We had no culture warriors in our corner. We weren't a constituency that had to be addressed. As I said, we were almost beyond the category of invisibility. Again, you first have to have a persistent presence to be ignored and rendered invisible, and the wider culture didn't even know we existed three dimensionally enough to be pushed aside and ignored.

On the day I finally got on the internet in 1999, I typed in "Arab American Theater" and found two or three organizations that specialized in my kind of stories. Two of those, the Arab Theatrical Arts Guild, and later, and with greater impact on my work, Golden Thread Productions, responded to my inquires.

Author's Note

The earliest of these pieces, an adaptation of Chekhov's A MARRIAGE PROPOSAL was done in February 2001 in Dearborn, Michigan at the Arab Theatrical Arts Guild. This Chekhov piece, with its universal themes of family, marriage and argument, is often adapted by different groups. Inserting Arabs into this play became a delicious, and truly radical act of counter-programming for me. "Here we goddamn are" was the motif playing in my head as I adapted this work. And here's the thing: throughout the various productions I've had of different short and full-length plays, I've noted that certain critics will critique my plays for having a political agenda (which is apparently a no-no, but that's a different discussion), when I rarely ever have an agenda of any kind when writing a play (except when writing satires, which by their very nature, have particular social and political targets in mind). But in the simple act of rendering a formally vilified and culturally absent group three-dimensionally, this very act of humanizing is seen as a political act. Which it is in a way, but not for the reasons they mean. An innocuous, non-political family matter would be seen as having a political agenda because representing a formally unseen group of people, in a way that makes them appear human, is seen as a shrill act of political activism. Even some of the most overtly "political" pieces here like THE MONOLOGIST SUFFERS HER MONOLOGUE is radical primarily because it gives voice to a character from a group that has repeatedly been silenced and ignored in American theater. Or, in the case of SO UNLIKE ME and THE SNIPER, to sentiments and ideas that aren't often given voice in mainstream theater.

Giving voice, rendering a formally flattened and despised people (when thought of at all) three dimensionally, and daring to want to occupy a little of that center stage, all these ordinary and basic acts become slapped with those much maligned "political" / "didactic" labels. People who walk into a space formally denied them will, by their every entrance, be seen as protestors protesting something.

It's a luxury to be above politics and the societal forces at play in a country. Not everyone can ignore the actions of governments, institutions, or people you might come across who express their prejudices either unabashedly, or conceal them in "facts and figures" and concern for your people's "problematic" (read "backward") culture. For those who can't ignore any of that, even if they wanted to, then all things domestic are bent towards the outside forces shaping their lives, i.e., the political. Your personal life becomes shaped by the stereotypes people have of you: again, as expressed either by government policy or by ordinary citizens whose prejudices don't allow you to continue your day as planned. So to dramatize all this in a play is actually to speak of *domestic* matters. Because politics at that point is in your very personal, churning gut, and in your very high blood pressure. You may want art to explore only existential concerns, or some universal themes like love, anger, ambition, etc. Or dabble in the high jinx and low points of the human condition. etc. And all these short pieces do that to some degree or another, but they also widen the frame and place their characters in the social and political context in which they operate. This, to me, is a more complete picture of the human condition. The political animal is the domestic animal is the human animal. It's not a case of one thing or the other.

So to the gatekeepers and the critics who dismiss these pieces and others like mine as no more than "political activism", ignoring everything else about them, and to

Author's Note

all those who want to return to the old programming, please, with all due respect, retire.

Because here's the other thing: I did not see myself represented on stage in the U S (or the U K, where I was raised) until my 40s. To repeat: not until my *40s* did I see any meaningful representation of Arabs, Muslims, Middle Easterners on stage. It took an accumulation of these kinds of short, and full length plays during the 2000s, by myself and others, to counter that particular void and insult.

FURTHER NOTES & ACKNOWLEDGMENTS

The earliest piece included ("A Marriage Proposal") is from 2001, the latest ("Radical Departure") is from 2021 and was presented over Zoom. I have resisted the temptation to rewrite the oldest pieces to update them, or conform more to my present writing style. They are what they are and are of their time.

I have limited information on a lot of these productions. It is the nature of short pieces to be folded into larger festivals, with often flyers for program notes which get lost. This is by way of apologizing to the wonderful crews, and behind-the-scenes folk who unfortunately will go unnamed because of my bad record keeping and faulty memory. You helped make these pieces, and the festivals they were in, shine. My thanks to all of you.

With some plays I have limited information for first productions, but no records for subsequent ones. With others I have records of multiple performances. So, sort of like a comb-over, I have listed those to make up for the bare spots in information on other productions.

I can't say these plays are listed with any discernible order. Some of these pieces like "So Unlike Me" and "The Sniper", and "Brass Knuckles" and "Radical Departure" are companion pieces. The former two I grouped together, the latter two bookend the collection. With the other pieces it was more a quick and dirty decision to place them in the order they're listed here.

My thanks to Michelle Mulholland, M Graham Smith and Hal Gelb for helping me gather the information needed to at least acknowledge the original actors for these pieces. And my thanks to Abdulrahmen "Ray" Alcodray and the Arab Theatrical Arts Guild for first staging A MARRIAGE PROPOSAL, and to Torange Yeghiazarian and Golden Thread Productions for being so supportive of my work over the years. Most of these short plays either received their world premiere, or were eventually staged by the theater Torange founded. Also thanks to A J Epstein and West of Lenin in Seattle for also supporting a couple of these works. And for the very last piece included, performed over Zoom, my thanks to Akin Salawu and Jerome Parker of the LIT council.

BRASS KNUCKLES

BRASS KNUCKLES was first performed at Cleveland Public Theatre's Station Hope Festival in 2018 under the title of KNUCKLEDUSTER. The cast and creative contributor were:

MAYSOON .... Maya Jones
Director .... M Graham Smith

BRASS KNUCKLES was later performed at Golden Thread Productions' ReOrient Festival in 2019 in San Francisco. The cast and creative contributor were:

MAYSOON .... Atosa Babaoff
Director .... Torange Yeghiazarian

CHARACTER

M<small>AYSOON</small>, *any age where the things she discusses can still hurt.*

(*A woman,* MAYSOON, *stands in front of a mirror [can be absent], facing the audience. She is dressed modestly. She proceeds to put on her hijab.*)

MAYSOON: Today I will go out and try again.

Today I will revisit the day I visited yesterday but with more confidence.

Today I will not scream.

I will not scream and freak people out.

If I do scream, I will make sure the scream has no spiky points.

It will not hurt me as it escapes my throat.

Nor will it hurt the person I am screaming at.

Today I will try and see the light in people's eyes.

I will pretend all the light in the world is there,

even if all I see are shark eyes.

Today I will think of God more.

I will make a space for him in my heart.

My heart will not crowd out God with useless anger.

I will not crowd out God by feeling all the feelings I usually feel that make me want to scream.

Today the sun is shining.

I've noticed it.

Good.

I will not stop feeling it's there even if the day starts clouding over, metaphorically speaking.

Today I will have more empathy for people who are assholes.

I will try and understand why they are that way. No:

Today I *won't* spend any time thinking about them.

To think about what makes a person an asshole is to sink into their mind-set. And do I really want to spend time in the mind of someone who has shit for brains?

That is nobody's life goal ever. Listen to me:

your only option is to avoid such people…

But—Maysoon—

sometimes rude, aggressive people are unavoidable.

You know that. So be prepared.

Try and avoid them, yes;

but, occasionally, out of nowhere, there they are in your face. With no inhibitions.

No filters to prevent the assholery that comes out of their mouths. So please: don't get sucked in.

Got it?

(Slight beat)

But what are you going to do if it happens again?

(Slight beat)

I'm asking, seriously.

(Slight beat. She considers her options.)

Not a clue.

You haven't started your day and already you're stuck in the negatives.

BRASS KNUCKLES

So today if someone tugs at my hijab on the bus, or on the street, or in a "I'm-only-kidding-kind-of-way", I will not take out my brass knuckles.

(She takes out brass knuckles from her pocket and slips them onto her fingers. She looks at them as if admiring jewelry.)

I will not take them out.

Perhaps alone—

in a bathroom stall—

after the impulse to take them out has passed.

To remind me of what I could have done.

But did not.

Because I didn't want to crowd out God from my heart.

The brass knuckles will be used as a reminder of the wrong path I could have taken...

were it not for God taking me by my brass knuckles hand and saying, "Maybe not? Maysoon...

"Maybe...?

"But maybe not?"

(She admires the brass knuckles on her fingers a little more, the empowered feeling she derives from them, before putting them back in her pocket.)

Today I will honor my self-defense instructor by *not* engaging the haters.

The first line of defense is walking away.

A woman with your credentials doesn't need to engage with someone whose only skills seem to be motor, and drooling.

You smile.

You walk away.

You confuse them with your sincere wish that they have a nice day. "Sir? I see you're clearly having a bad day. I truly hope it gets better. And God bless you. God bless *you*".

And then just walk. —Walk away.

A simple "God bless you" is more effective than a hammer to the knee caps.

They will be floored by your smile.

Who needs brass knuckles when love can pierce the heart. Really—

deeply—

pierce the heart.

And twist.

Just...let God's love twist in there.

Love is not weakness.

Love is a weapon.

Fuck up their day with love.

But you have to mean it sincerely otherwise it won't work.

Which means you can't get any satisfaction when you see their mouths drop.

Or, Inshallah, doubled up in the agony of their own ignorance. By a gut-punch from love.

(Slight beat)

Thank you—Maysoon—for trying to be grown up about this.

And may I say you are looking especially nice today. And I don't mean that in a vain, *Kardashian* kind of way.

(Or whoever the current pop or reality-TV star is.)

Why wear this if you're not going to at least *try* and honor God?

Do you wear this to escape the treadmill of the latest fashions? No.

You do it to remember God.

And you can do that by behaving calmly, honorably.

Never stooping down to the level of the people who insult you. *Why* they feel the need to insult you, who cares. That's their business.

Yes, they are holes filled primarily with fecal matter, aka assholes, but that's their punishment.

You could be a saint and try and relieve them of their poop-filled qualities,

but you already have a full-time job.

One day, maybe, God will give you the patience to be a full-time ambassador of His.

But right now…focus on not reacting.

And remember, in the first law of thermodynamics, that which is fucked-up about people can neither be created anew nor destroyed.

There are a limited number of awful people out there and that's all. You may one day grow into someone who can change people's minds—but you're not there yet.

Not by a long shot.

You feel…

you feel too much.

You hurt—too easily.

Focus on not hurting today.

Focus on not hurting.

Don't flinch.

Don't bleed.

Don't break down and cry.

Don't—just—don't embarrass me.

Please.

I can't keep patching you up everyday. It's...it's too exhausting.

(Slight beat)

Maysoon:

You are a good person.

I'm not just saying that.

Well—I am.

Because most days I want to scream. In a very uncharitable way.

Can you be a good person and be angry all the time?...

I don't know. I'm asking.

Good people rise above it all, don't they?

Isn't that what's special about good people?

They float above that thin film of scum that seems to coat everything? "Oh, look at Elizabeth, she's so nice to everyone. She always has a smile for you. So gracious. Such dignity. Elizabeth is genuinely a good person".

One day I will be Elizabeth....

One day.

But today I will settle for me.

The best version of myself.

So repeat after me:

Today I will not hurt...

(Slight beat)

"I will not hurt."

I will not cry.

"I will not cry."

I will not scream.

…"I will not scream."

Today I will try and see the good in everyone.

…"Today I will try and see the good in everyone."

(Slight beat)

Inshallah.

(Then, she closes her eyes, opens her palms in prayer and recites:)

"Bismillah al Rahman al Raheem."

(She opens her eyes and looks at herself…. She takes out lipstick and applies it. She pockets the lipstick. She pats the pocket with the brass knuckles. Still there. Good. She smiles—unrelated to the brass knuckles. She looks at herself. She takes a deep breath.)

Hello day. I'm ready for you.

Are you ready for me?

(Slight beat. Blackout)

END OF PLAY

PICKING UP THE SCENT

PICKING UP THE SCENT was first performed at Golden Thread Productions' ReOrient Festival in 2015 in San Francisco. The cast and creative contributor were:

NISRIN...Nora El Samahy
HISHAM ....Damien Seperi
ANNABEL...Roneet Aliza Rahamim

Director... Evren Odcikin

CHARACTERS

NISRIN, *20s or 30s*
HISHAM, *20s or 30s*
ANNABEL, *20s or 30s*

(*Lights up on a woman,* NISRIN, *at a table. She picks up a perfume bottle. She looks at it. She sprays a little on her wrist. She smells it. Light change. A man,* HISHAM, *enters, as she rubs the scented wrist on her neck. He wraps his arms around her and nuzzles his nose close to her neck. He makes an appreciative noise as he takes in the scent.*)

HISHAM: I have good taste.

NISRIN: What's the occasion?

HISHAM: Do I need a reason to give my wife a present?

NISRIN: It's lovely. —Citrus. Lemon trees and a picnic…cool shades.

HISHAM: What else? What else does it remind you of?

NISRIN: It reminds me my husband is a very thoughtful individual. Who usually buys me presents when he has bad news to tell me.

HISHAM: I'm offended. We haven't been married long enough for me to be that predictable. I'm a little harder to read, surely.

NISRIN: It's why I married you. You're an easy read. Like a cheap romance novel. The kind you pick up at the airport.

HISHAM: Okay, now you're just being insulting. I'm a lot more mysterious than that. If we're talking books, compare me to a good mystery novel at the very least. Men in trench coats under street lights. Beautiful women spotted through upstairs windows.

NISRIN: A mystery, huh?

HISHAM: The kind where the woman comes to the private eye for help. She comes in wearing some beautiful scent he can't stop thinking about after she leaves. He takes the case for that reason alone. He wants to follow the scent, literally. He wants to keep breathing it in.

(HISHAM *holds* NISRIN *again.*)

NISRIN: Isn't there usually some unpleasant secret in mystery novels? What are you keeping from me?

HISHAM: We don't want to take the analogy too far.

NISRIN: Hisham?

HISHAM: I'm more about the trench coats and the beautiful women.

NISRIN: Just tell me. —What's going on?

(*Slight beat.* HISHAM *takes a breath:*)

HISHAM: Okay…now…don't get upset.

NISRIN: I knew it.

HISHAM: No gnashing of teeth allowed.

NISRIN: I'm already gnashing. What is it?

HISHAM: Just remember the perfume bottle.

(NISRIN *levels a look at* HISHAM, *urging him to spill. Then:*)

HISHAM: I'm going to help Hassan at the archaeological site.

(NISRIN *looks at* HISHAM. *Then moves away from him.*)

NISRIN: You do want to play the hero.

HISHAM: No. I would just like to do my job.

NISRIN: (*Reining in her emotions*) A job, Hisham, is something you go to with a good idea you'll return from at the end of the day. You go in, say hi to your co-workers. You gossip about what you saw on T V the night before. A few hours of work and then you come home.

HISHAM: All of which I plan to do.

NISRIN: Really? War notwithstanding. The bombs won't magically affect you. Because, why? They affect others, not you? Your Ph.D in archaeology somehow protects you?

HISHAM: The fighting hasn't reached the site yet.

NISRIN: You're taking the word of our government paid mouthpieces who call themselves journalists?

HISHAM: Now's the time to go before it really gets bad.

NISRIN: Their thugs are already there kidnapping and killing people. Whole neighborhoods are gone. They're laying the groundwork for a full scale assault.

HISHAM: And before that assault rolls in, we need to rescue as many artifacts as we can.

NISRIN: "Rescue." You talk of it as some life saving mission. These are scraps from another time you're going after. They're not worth losing your life over.

HISHAM: It's our history, Nisrin, which I'm very proud of. Do I put down your study of poetry?

NISRIN: I wouldn't risk my life over it.

HISHAM: It's important enough for you to go all the way to London to study it.

NISRIN: Is this what this is about? My going abroad to study? You're going to get back at me by going off to some war zone?

HISHAM: It's not a war zone yet.

NISRIN: "Yet." In about two seconds. And you don't need actual tanks to call it a war.

HISHAM: In those two seconds you can uncover a whole lot.

NISRIN: Seriously, is this about me pursuing my studies?

HISHAM: That's the second insult today.

NISRIN: Is it?

HISHAM: I *want* you to go. I believe in your passion. Why can't you support mine?

NISRIN: Because the only thing *I* might die from is boredom in class. If armed men were roaming the halls of London University picking off students, or bombs were falling on King's Cross, no, I wouldn't go. I wouldn't subject you to that worry. I'd study my poetry elsewhere, like any sane person.

HISHAM: You can pursue your passion where you want. Mine is pretty site-specific. I have to be there. Nisrin, Hassan is uncovering amazing things already. An entire domestic dwelling intact. Whole inscriptions. He's piecing together what life was like almost three thousand years ago for ordinary people. This is too important to ignore.

NISRIN: So wait until things calm down and then go.

HISHAM: Nobody's going to cordon off that area and tell the combatants to kill themselves somewhere else. *(Slight beat)*
You know what really infuriates me about war? Apart from, you know, people getting killed who have no business dying so horribly and too soon. Is that you realize there's no one at the steering wheel of this great big fuck-up called war. I don't know why I expect there to be some kind of intelligence when everyone's going nuts. But I do. Then you realize, wait, there isn't because it's *war*. Which means everyone's checked their brain at the door. And what everyone seems to be doing at this point is just managing a catastrophe. Nisrin, we have to save what we can, while we can.

They won't get to rob us of our history. They may be fucking up our present and our future, but they don't get to destroy our heritage. *Our* history.

NISRIN: *(Agitated)* Okay, just—

HISHAM: I wish Hassan had left the site buried, but now that it's visible, it'll be used to shoot from, and fight around, which means firepower is going to target that area.

NISRIN: Fine, you're going. I don't need to hear all your reasonable arguments for doing what will still be a stupid thing to do.

(Beat)

HISHAM: You're a poet. You have to understand. —To step into another time. Figure out what life was like for ordinary people. Kings and queens live on, but do we get to resurrect lives like ours? And be able to tell their stories again? ...I have a great job: I help bring back the dead.

NISRIN: You don't need to be a poet to point out the irony there. There's a greater chance of you joining them than you bringing anyone back from the grave.

(Slight beat)

HISHAM: I love the fact that you're going to study abroad. I admire you for pursuing what you love. The way you fought to get the visas. Found a place to stay. How you met every obstacle with an attitude of "that's not going to stop me". Between the war, and family expectations, everything around you is telling you to shut up and hide. But you said "screw that".

NISRIN: You sure I'm not running away? Getting out of the country when others can't?

HISHAM: You're standing up for what you believe in. And doing it when everything's going to hell; which is exactly the time to stand up for what you believe in.

NISRIN: Silly little poems. —Against all that.

HISHAM: Especially during this time. Each of those poems, writing them, studying them, each line: it's a glorious middle finger to those who would steal everything decent and good from us. They do everything they can to bury us in their savagery. Maybe we can't bring down the tyrants alone, but I won't be made to feel even more helpless by being turned away from what I love. This is how I resist. How we both do. You with your poetry, me with my... my ruins.

(NISRIN *looks at* HISHAM, *then:*)

NISRIN: It's four months from now.... I'm remembering you.... And I think I've lost you.

HISHAM: What?

(*Light change. Sound of an airport. Duty Free shop.*
ANNABEL *enters. She wears an outfit appropriate for her job as an airport sales person.* HISHAM *maintains his gaze on* NISRIN *for a second, then exits.*)

ANNABEL: One of my favorites. "Elysian."
(*She picks up the perfume bottle and sprays a little on a stick of paper.*)
It smells of all things summer, doesn't it? Picnics, cool shades. A perfect blend for hotter climates.
(*She smells it.*)
You don't want something too clingy or musky. Something light as linen for these summer months. Are you interested in purchasing a bottle, madam?

NISRIN: *(Distracted)* What?

ANNABEL: Would you like me to wrap a bottle for you?

NISRIN: I dropped mine. When I first came.

ANNABEL: Dropped?

NISRIN: *(Still speaking as if half present, half somewhere else)* I had a bottle of this perfume. When I first came to London. A present from my husband. It slipped out of my hand in the bathroom.

ANNABEL: Oh. I'm sorry. Lucky for you we stock it.

NISRIN: My whole flat smelled of it for weeks. You could smell it in the hallway. It made me laugh. To think what others must have thought of me. "Look at that foreign woman, drowning herself in perfume."

ANNABEL: There's nothing wrong walking around smelling nice. Not in my book.

NISRIN: *(Still distracted by the memory)* It was as if he were home. When I smelt that. I would return to my flat and I'd imagine he'd come on a surprise visit. As if it was his cologne.

ANNABEL: *(Confused)* Sorry?

NISRIN: My husband.

ANNABEL: Oh; right. His present.

NISRIN: My husband's an archeologist.

ANNABEL: Oh yes?

NISRIN: He digs up ruins. He brings back the dead. That's the way he likes to think of it.

ANNABEL: That sounds exciting.

NISRIN: I think he's been murdered.

(Light change.)

NISRIN: I'm going to my lectures, Hisham. I'm so thrilled to be here. To sit and listen to my professors talk about Edmund Spenser and John Donne. Milton. Dryden. I think I'm in heaven. To spend my days studying such writers. To think of nothing but syntax and grammar. Rhythm, meter, and genius. You were right, this is my kind of resistance. And when they speak of war—when it's mentioned in relation to some of these writers, it feels unreal. As if there couldn't possibly be any violence associated with these great works. It's only a description of blood. A pool of words, words spilled, not real blood. It's only when I go home and smell your perfume that I remember. And that pool of words turns back into real blood. — Listening to the news…. Why didn't you come with me? I should have pleaded. If only so I wouldn't feel so damn guilty now for these wonderful moments of forgetting.

(Light change.)

ANNABEL: Madam? Are you alright?

(Another light change. HISHAM *enters. Perhaps he appears a little dusty, as if he's been digging. He carries a very small jar/container. Very faint sounds of war—gun fire, an explosion—will play at a couple of points as he speaks.)*

HISHAM: Look at what we've found. In my bones I'm sure I know what it is, even though Hassan says we can't jump to any conclusions. Look at the attached photo. I'm pretty sure it's a jar that held a fragrance. Lilies are mentioned everywhere in stone inscriptions. I wouldn't be surprised if the area had an ancient perfumery. I can almost smell the fragrance it held. I know that's totally my imagination, but we'll be able to run tests. Can you believe it if it's true?

NISRIN: Hisham.

HISHAM: Coming here has been so worth it.

NISRIN: Where are you? You're not responding to my emails.

HISHAM: Everything confirms this site was someone's home. I'm going crazy, in a good way, imagining the lives of the people who lived here. I'm terrified all this might be blown to pieces before we can collect everything and get an idea of who these people were. I feel like I'm at an operating table and I have just minutes left trying to save someone's life before the bombs fall on us.

(Light change.)

NISRIN: *(As if on the phone)* Hisham? Can you hear me?

HISHAM: *(As if on the phone)* Nisrin? How are you enjoying London?

NISRIN: *(As if on the phone)* I can barely hear you. What was that?

(Re: faint sound of an explosion)

HISHAM: *(As if on the phone)* It's nothing.

NISRIN: *(As if on the phone)* That sounded like an explosion. Was that an explosion?

HISHAM: *(As if on the phone)* Don't worry. The rebels here said we're safe.

NISRIN: *(As if on the phone)* Hisham, I can't hear you.

HISHAM: *(As if on the phone)* Hello?

NISRIN: *(As if on the phone)* Hisham?

(Light change. Spot back on NISRIN. HISHAM, along with ANNABEL [now as the woman HISHAM describes], remain in the dark.)

NISRIN: The strangest thing is happening: …I'm starting to see everything through your eyes. I walk the streets of London and feel like an archeologist. I see the whole of London like it's long been buried and I am recreating it in my mind's eye. Everything feels like it's covered in ash. As if some terrible cataclysm has befallen this city. And I do what you do: I try and bring the site back to life. Only I don't know what I'm trying to recover since it's all there right in front of me.

(Lights up on HISHAM *next to "*ANNABEL*".)*

HISHAM: I hold this fragrance jar and imagine the woman who might have held it.

*("*ANNABEL*" takes the jar from* HISHAM *and does what he describes.)*

NISRIN: London's turned to ash. Ash in the food I taste. Ash in my eyes.

HISHAM: She pours a little out and rubs it on her wrists. Along her neck.

(A little laugh)

Don't get jealous, Nisrin, but I think I'm falling in love with this woman. She's a little old for me at over two thousand years. But she's really firing up my imagination.

NISRIN: I'm starting to look at everyone as if I'm seeing them before the cataclysm. Before their lives changed forever. The nightlife, the laughing. Their ignorance of what's happening around the edges of their lives. How dare they talk of stupid stuff like music and movies when five hours away by plane the world is ending.

HISHAM: Maybe she's getting ready for her lover. Her husband's been away too long and she's forced to find affection elsewhere. So of course I have to be her lover since I'm the one creating this scenario.

NISRIN: You've robbed me of my pleasure, Hisham. You told me to go and throw myself into my poetry but I keep getting dragged back. *You* drag me back with worry. And all I'm tasting is the dirt you're sifting through. This isn't resistance anymore. I can't fight back the way we talked about. All I can think of is the war and that no one's paying attention. Not even you it seems.

HISHAM: Our imagination is something else, isn't it? This little artifact. The way it's opened a whole new world for me.

NISRIN: Where are you, Hisham? Stop what you're doing and find a way to reach me.

HISHAM: I'm sending a letter with this English journalist. I want you to know I've never been more excited and you shouldn't worry. Last night I had the best dream. I think it's a reward for spending so much energy trying to imagine the lives of the people who lived here. Especially this woman I keep seeing. I won't go into the whole dream in case you get jealous, but she started to speak to me.

("ANNABEL" turns to him as if she wants to tell HISHAM something.)

HISHAM: As if this woman made a special trip to tell me her story. She seemed so full of joy and wanted to speak of her life. But stupid gunfire woke me up.

NISRIN: Hisham!

HISHAM: *(Irritated)* What?

(Light change that isolates NISRIN and HISHAM. They speak directly to each other now. "ANNABEL" has exited.)

NISRIN: Where have you been?

HISHAM: Where else would I be?

NISRIN: I've been frantically trying to reach you. Your family's been frantically trying to reach you.

HISHAM: You've found me. How's London?

NISRIN: You can't ask me how London is like nothing's the matter. I'm worried sick!

HISHAM: I'm *fine*. Hassan's fine. We're doing great work. Did you get my letter?

NISRIN: What letter?

HISHAM: I sent you a letter with a journalist.

NISRIN: Did you get any of my emails?

HISHAM: Everything's down. Most of the computer guys in this town have joined the rebels. If you want your computer fixed you have to go to the front lines. Hassan's assistant went, but he had his computer clipped by enemy fire. The rebels were so mad, they said they'd fix it for free. I'm glad we're on the side of the tech guys here.

NISRIN: I'm so angry with you right now I could hit you.

HISHAM: I'm *sorry*. How have you been?

NISRIN: I'm telling you!

HISHAM: Tell me about London.

NISRIN: I'm not able to enjoy anything anymore! My joy lasted for about two minutes. I hate the fact that people walk around oblivious about our suffering.

HISHAM: You can't blame them.

NISRIN: Of course I can't, but I'm doing it anyway.

HISHAM: Did you try their fish and chips yet?

NISRIN: I don't want to talk about fish and chips!

HISHAM: Did you go to Marks and Spencer and get the prawn sandwich?

NISRIN: Hisham!

HISHAM: Okay, but remember to bring that cake back with you, the one with the pink squares and the marzipan.

NISRIN: Does that mean I'm going to see you? Soon?

HISHAM: God-willing. Just a little while longer.

NISRIN: You could have all the cake and sandwiches you want if you came to London.

HISHAM: I'm sorry I'm putting you through this. I can't tell you what a relief it is to know you're safe out of the country.
(Cutting her off before she can respond.)
I know, it's not fair that I can't do the same for you. But we've just scratched the surface. They've peeled off some fighters to protect the site, but it's only a matter of time before the fighting makes its way to this spot.

NISRIN: Please don't get cocky just because the worst hasn't happened.

HISHAM: I know it must be harder for you, being anxious all the time.

NISRIN: I think you like the attention.

HISHAM: I do; but we're both where we need to be. More than ever I believe we should spend what time we have doing what we love. And yes, also being with who we love, *you*. But I've spent too much of my life living with so much fear. I'm so mad that we've—that *I've* allowed that to happen. That I've let these monsters have such power over me. And because I did, my first fight has to be with this terror that's made such a coward of me. I have…I have seen so much good in this town. People aren't scared anymore. You wouldn't believe the light in people's eyes now.

(HISHAM and NISRIN look at each other.)

NISRIN: I want to come to you.

HISHAM: Didn't you hear what I said? You need to be doing what you love now more than ever. Write more poetry. Enjoy the hell out of London.

NISRIN: Wait…how can I be touching you?

HISHAM: Why would the laws of physics apply here?

NISRIN: Here?

(NISRIN *opens* HISHAM's *jacket. She sees a large patch of blood on his shirt.*)

NISRIN: Oh no. Oh no.

HISHAM: That gun fire that woke me up? From my beautiful dream about the woman holding the perfume jar? It tore right through the wall where my bed was…I know that woman was trying to tell me something.

NISRIN: Oh Hisham.

HISHAM: Don't worry, it didn't hurt. It happened too quickly to hurt.

NISRIN: Are you…? I don't know what this is. —Are you dead? —Am I dreaming this?

HISHAM: I'm not sure, to be honest.

NISRIN: I'm coming.

HISHAM: Please don't do that.

NISRIN: I'm getting on a plane and coming to you.

HISHAM: It's too dangerous now. Wait until the fighting has stopped.

NISRIN: I'm coming to find you.

HISHAM: Nisrin. Wait.

(*Light change. Airport sounds.* HISHAM *exits.*)

ANNABEL: Madam? —Are you alright? —Would you like me to get someone from customer service?

NISRIN: No… No, I'm fine. I have to go.

ANNABEL: (*Regarding the perfume*) Will you be taking a bottle with you?

NISRIN: No. I can't stand that smell now.

PICKING UP THE SCENT

(NISRIN *exits.* ANNABEL *looks at the perfume. She brings it to her nose and breathes in the fragrance. Light change.* ANNABEL *now speaks as the woman* HISHAM *spoke of, the one who may have owned the fragrance jar. If she had a scarf around her neck, she now drapes it over her head.)*

ANNABEL: *(Woman from the past)* What I started to say to you before you woke up….
What I wanted to tell you was, simply—thank you. Thank you for being so passionate about wanting to find out about me. Who knew I would have an admirer after all this time. After I had turned to dust.
Everything passes…everything passed so quickly. Each moment swallowed by the next, and the next. Life gone in a second. And here you are trying to piece it together. Imagining the pieces; the links between your time and mine.
The jar you found held lilies, Hisham. Oils, and herbs. I would make my own fragrances. I would sell them to all the travelers who passed through our city. Assyrians, Egyptians. Persians, Phoenicians. All the different tribes who passed through here. I sold these amazing fragrances to all those tired travelers.
But then the wars came. So much bloodletting. Such madness. I don't know what drives people to go over such cliffs in their souls.
Hisham: —Don't stop digging. I'll tell you more the more you unearth. Hisham, please, don't stop looking for me.
Find me.
(Blackout)

END OF PLAY

THE TYRANT

THE TYRANT was first performed as part of Sandbox Artists Collective's "SOAPfest" at the West of Lenin Theater in Seattle in 2014. The cast and creative contributor were:

HABIB.. G Valmont Thomas
Director ....Anita Montgomery

CHARACTER

HABIB, *anywhere from late 40s to 70s*

(*An empty stage apart from a chair, a projector, and a table with a pitcher of water and a glass. HABIB is present when the lights go up. He wears a suit. He surveys the audience. Then:*)

HABIB: (*Accent*) In this fox hunt, it would appear the hounds have gathered around me…. And how happy you all seem to be. A guilty pleasure, I'm sure. Invited to attend this, what would you call this? And from which you're meant to—what exactly? Learn? I think this is the point of the exercise today. You have come to observe. This observation being part of my punishment. Don't be embarrassed if you're just here to gloat. I understand the attraction in that. I have done the same. Been much too pleased in the discomfort of people I have not seen eye-to-eye with. And yes, as it has been reported, I would sometimes go into the prison cells of my enemies and point out to them that they are not where they hoped to be.

Seeing one's enemy fall is really a lovely feeling.

It is such a pleasure, in fact, that if you have no enemies, I would suggest you go out and make some. And then do something to bring them to their knees. Really. It is so much better than sex. To be full of such righteousness in dealing with an enemy. And then to believe that righteousness exists for the sake of other people, a whole nation?

It is no longer personal revenge, you see. You're doing it for the good of the country. Tyrants, if this is what I am now called, are actually, if you will follow this reasoning for a second, overly helpful people. In that they are willing to shoulder so much. To the point where, yes, people may feel bullied by that helpfulness. Your helpfulness *can* overstay its welcome….

So I would like to begin this by saying, yes, I became too full with this hubris of feeling I was doing good for other people. And from this arrogance, I became—shall we say, blind to a number of things? Let me write this down.

(He goes to the projector and writes with a black marker.)

You'll be surprised by how truthful I will be with you today. I only ask that you show me the same honesty in return.

(Writes: "Arrogance/Hubris".)

I am sorry this projector is an antique. I have to tell you, your prisons here: not so much. My observations of how you punish people doesn't really say good things about you, to be frank. With the amount of bullshit I heard from you about human rights, I had imagined a very different place. There, "arrogance, hubris". First confession.

And let me say this: though they have said my honesty today will decide my final sentencing, it is not for that reason I will be frank. In being honest about myself, I must tell you…I will have to be honest about you too. They could not have dragged me out here if it was just to make a public spectacle of myself. I came out here to make a public spectacle of you too. So be warned, you are part of this story.

Now…at first I think, why not like Cleopatra? She would not allow herself to be paraded down the streets of Rome. A queen forced to kneel before her new master? Impossible. We see what happened with the last dictator you went to war with. You find him in a

THE TYRANT

hole and then parade him on T V with a doctor shining a light into his mouth like he is cattle, or a slave. I think, Habib, this is not for you. I ask, is it fear of death that prevents me from putting a gun to my head?

No. Death is not what scares me. What scares me most is that I sink into history without a proper accounting of what is what. You and me need to settle accounts before you bury me in this dust-bin of history.

And don't worry: I know I am famous for making four hour speeches but this will be a very short one as I have been given a time limit. Plus, they serve dinner at a strict time here with no exceptions. Also, please know that I hold no anger towards you individually. I know I could laugh with each one of you if we were alone together. I love Americans. You are a unique species. The rest of us, we live on a different planet, but you: you occupy the space of the elected. For the moment, anyway. Tomorrow, who knows. You may end up feeling what we feel. But for now, you are, how shall I put this: you are not…your insides are not quite bruised in the way ours are. This block we go around, you have not been around it as many times as we have. For over five thousand years of recorded history we have gone around this block. We built the fucking block. But you, you feel a little separate from all this, no?

My gift to you this evening is to please feel this superiority freely, without guilt. Do not let your high moral standards interfere with the enjoyment of watching another man squirm in front of you. And for those of you who might sympathize with me, to see a human being, never mind a former leader of a people, to see a human being have his dignity stripped away from him. No worries. I used to tell my opponents, those times I would hear of them being asked to give us information in ways they said were painful, undignified, I would say to them, we have aspirin for the pain. And for dignity, it is something you either have, or you don't. Nobody can take that away from you. If you scream and beg for mercy, that is you being you. I am man enough to stand under the glare of your contempt. You can not strip me of anything because I know who I am. For instance, if you madam—

(To someone in the audience.)

—wanted to slap me in the face, you could do so. You will see I am the same man before and after the slap. There would be no loss of dignity for me.

(Gets close to her.)

In fact, please be so kind as to go ahead and slap me. Permission given.

(A large red light flashes on, accompanied by a glaring sound.)

Ah.

Not allowed. It seems we have a referee for my talk with you this evening. No matter. But just so you know, as much as some people want to see me humbled like a dog, it can not happen. On the other hand,

(Again, close to the audience.)

if I was to slap one of you, I think you would crumble like that:

(He snaps his fingers. Again, the red light comes on accompanied by the sound, He backs away.)

And why is this? Why am I able to stand my ground regardless of what you do to me? Humbly I would suggest, and this will sound more like this arrogance I have just confessed to, it is because, and I do not say the word lightly, "Destiny"—

(He lets the word sink in.)

THE TYRANT 41

Destiny tapped *me* on my shoulder, and not you. Trust me, this is not a gift. If Destiny passes you by, then give God thanks. For to be a leader is to be like an ox burdened with a yoke. It is funny to me that in this time of my greatest humiliation, when I am to stand before you like a beaten servant, it is to tell you that my calling was, to *be a servant*. Destiny said, "Habib: your life-calling is very simple: you will serve others for the rest of your life. Not the playboy you want to be. No: you are to humble yourself before your people". This is what I have felt all my life.

And like a servant, my masters, my people, chose to spit on me. And beat me. And accuse me of treating them like shit, when I was the one swallowing all the shit on their behalf, *your* shit, that you shoveled into my country, for thirty plus years I swallowed on their behalf. And now this…. But I am not crushed by this. You can not crush me. Because a servant stands and falls with his master. They do not understand that when they slap me, my people slap themselves right back. They really don't know what they've done. The ungrateful little "hamars".

That's "donkeys" in English.

I serve them and they bend me over? Well my message back to them is very simple: fuck you too. Let me write that down:

(He writes: "Fuck you too, Love, your President". He says the words as he writes them:)

Fuck—you—too. Love—your President.

(To the audience)

And you too, to be honest. You live in this perfect bubble called America but you get to live in this bubble because of people like me. I am your man overseas. I protect you from the mad fanatics who say *you're* the problem. I say, fuck you too.

(Speaks the words as he writes them:)

Fuck you, America, you ungrateful little cocksuckers.

(He heavily underlines the word "cocksuckers".)

Enough.

I don't want to lose my cool here. Let's keep this pleasant.

And on top of everything I'm not allowed to smoke. Well aren't you all just so healthy. Please excuse me if I occasionally sink into "Third World" negativity. Sometimes your perfectly enlightened ideas feels like red fire ants crawling up my ass. Enough.

(Slight beat)

Back to me being made an example of...for your edification.

(He will either wipe away the "fuck you's", or remove the transparency sheet on which they've been written. Now he writes "I served my people".)

"Service." Yes. What could he mean, the liar. Surrounding himself with all that pomp and ceremony and then daring to say he served his people. Riding around in limousines with whole roads closed off so he can pass by. When was the last time a servant ever commanded an army, or had his picture hung everywhere?

About that. My portraits.

There've been complaints that my image was always everywhere you looked in my country. Billboards, offices, streets.

(Either using the slide projector, or a clicker for an off-stage projector, he projects an image of his outsized portrait.)

THE TYRANT

First of all, am I so ugly that that's a problem? Does this face make your stomach turn?

(Another portrait is shown.)

Wouldn't someone look at that instead and think: I can go to bed feeling at ease tonight knowing someone is watching over me? Not *everyone* has a television or computer. I'm sorry we have to use such blunt advertising. But that's what these are: advertisements for the service I provide. They are saying, where ever you are, I'm here to serve you. Or my team is. I will admit that in practice this makes me out to be a megalomaniac.

But it only seems like megalomania if you're not used to it. In my country, this is like hanging a family portrait up. All over the house. A reminder that I *am* like a big brother, or a father. Baba. And you *can* count on me to be there for you. We're very emotional in my country. We like to feel close to each other. We don't have this Western attitude of every man for himself. Here, you celebrate the individual. The cowboy alone on his horse.

(Mimics a cowboy)

The hero, by himself, riding alone into the sunset. Everyone's alone here. No wonder pharmaceuticals grow big with all the depression this brings on. We may be miserable for other reasons but at least we're miserable together. And so the need for these portraits. Which are really of the office I hold, not of me per se.

Now: this has led people to say I am too much like a father, treating our citizens like kids. *And?* Would you let your child drive a car before he's ready? We have too much illiteracy and ignorance where I'm from. Those in the know need to be responsible and lead their big family out of this ignorance. Otherwise

I would rightly be accused of being an irresponsible father, and letting anarchy rule our house.

The other way is your way, of course. You—not you, your government, they treat you like statistics. Everything is cold and unloving in your country. You put on the smiling face and say welcome, but really you're showing people out the door all the time. Look, there is a simple difference between our peoples that you need to know: We *like* strong leaders where I come from. We *know* we live in a dangerous neighborhood. We want someone who can kick the ass when necessary. We want "baba", or papa, because we want to know we're safe. And like all good fathers everywhere…sometimes I had to be strict. And so to these accusations of torture and human rights abuses, etc. Let me get to that.

(Perhaps takes a sip of water)

Do you mind if I leave these up?

(One or two portraits remain projected onto the wall. It could be more, though it could also just be one portrait, in which case "these" would be changed to "this".)

This is not vanity. There is just no visual stimulation in my prison cell. You really are more advanced when it comes to torture. Really, you have my respect. I have been taking mental notes of your well researched techniques for breaking a man down. We never had the funds to explore such exquisite methods. But I approve, it's working. I don't feel quite myself. Imprison a man alone long enough and he will jump at a chance to fraternize even with his own lynch mob. It's really amazing how you Americans continue to celebrate your values, when your misdeeds make the people you accuse of war crimes look like amateurs. I am in awe of your self-delusion. You are unhappy with your lying politicians but still you have faith

THE TYRANT

in your own goodness. Slavery, the genocide of the Natives, the wars you wage. I would respectfully ask you, at what point do you good people become liable for the crimes done in your name? By the people you elect. I don't mean to point the finger when we seem to be getting on so well but you are here to shove a broomstick up my ass, so to speak. I would like to break that broomstick in half and share it with you.

Speaking of which:

(Perhaps he takes another sip of water)

a videotape was released showing an officer of mine shoving a stick up a prisoner's anus. Also, other images of people suffering at the hands of my security forces. Alright. I will dispense with the weakest excuse but it's true: there are those in this audience who perhaps run big companies. Do you always know what your employees are up to? You're liable for their actions, yes, but do you know? I know this is the argument of a weak leader so I won't press it. But I would hear of the actions of my security forces *sometimes*, and I would say to the people who do this, "Really? This is what you do when you run out of ideas? What are you, a child, that you go to the poopy area? Or you try and drown a man? Or electrocute him?" I am personally against this. I know I said bringing an enemy to their knees is a pleasure but less so if you do it with a stick. Using the mind to break a man apart, that is using your imagination. By means of the mind: that civilizes the art of persuasion from something barbaric to something that would not offend even you. Even "violence" has its do's and don'ts. *Do* try and make the man cooperate. *Don't* be an animal as you go about doing it. We don't have the money to fully train people like you, but your way is our ideal. The way you simply strip a man naked, put him in a cramped cell alone, make him stand for extended periods, tying his limbs, stressing them with surgical hits, keeping a bright light on with music blaring; slamming him into walls, this is the way to do it. Do this for weeks, months, even a few days, and he's no longer a man. We aspire to be like you in many ways, and hope one day we will leave our childish sticks and stones and adopt your more refined methods.

Now:

(Using the clicker, he removes his portraits.)

to the heart of the matter: Do you seriously think there aren't people out there who want to hurt you? You Americans. In the West. Hurt you, badly.

Of course you know this. There are people in this world who want to extinguish your lives. Why? Because. Fill in the blanks. Because you're everywhere. Your pop culture is everywhere. Your naked buttocks and boobies are in their social feeds. They feel your values are shoved down their throats. You offend them. You offend their religion; or you bomb them and invade them. Blah blah, whatever. There *is* a boogeyman. He is not a fantasy of some corrupt politician out to stir the crowds for votes. You want the real world to be filled with grays and ambiguity, and things you can discuss over wine. In reality, sorry to inform you, there are people who hesitate only in wondering how to kill you. Knife, gun or bomb? Which is the more macho? They truly want to attack us. You and me. I put myself in your company because, well, were it not for the fact that I am your prisoner, I'm sure I would be your dinner guest. We are political allies. You can not appreciate that because of the lies you've been told about me, but never mind that now. I know some of you think you can sit down with these people and talk them out of their bad thoughts. Or persuade them to put aside their bombs and discuss their

THE TYRANT

concerns over a cappuccino. Everyone is redeemable, you think, yes? Surely we don't live in Hollywood films where villains plot and rub their hands in glee at the evil they have planned?

It is the nature of privilege, yours, to think this way. I applaud you for it. We want your ideas of utopia to poke our real world now and again. I am a big supporter of the arts; and the imagination. These portraits you saw were actually commissions. But while you dream up symphonies and poetry there is someone like me who must guard the gates of your homes and cinemas, because some people take great offense at your free thinking. You think *my* censorship was bad. Wait until you see what these guys want to ban. And I only censored to keep the peace. But these people? They hate the very things that make life worth living for us. They think, and I'm sorry I return to the image of the anus, so there might be something to my team's fixation on this area, but it's like their whole life is this tightly locked asshole and they want to project that onto the rest of us. They want to lock up life and bury it. They're afraid of it, of fresh ideas, the free spirit. These people want to tell you what to think, how to conduct the smallest things of your life. They don't want you to be you. They want you to be them. Liberty? It makes them pee in their pants. Really:

(He holds up a fist to indicate a tight sphincter.)

They are the sphincters of life. Perhaps I'm wrong to think my men were brutes. Perhaps they are good psychiatrists applying a kind of physical therapy to open these men up.

I helped keep these fanatics away from my people, and from *you*.

(Let's that settle, then:)

It is a tricky business fighting fire with fire. And yes, fire will sometimes leap the fence and hurt those you don't intend to hurt. And the difference between good fire and bad is hard to distinguish sometimes. One of my favorite quotes, "When you stare into the abyss, the abyss stares back at you" is true. Staring into the abyss: it will hurt you.

But this is the burden I took on while my people worked to put food on their table. It was my job to take on this darkness threatening them, knowing I will be touched by it. And I was. You should have seen me before all this. I was the life of the party. And charming. And sweet. I was like Mary Poppins. With a security service. In fact I am more like all the characters Julie Andrews ever played than anything you might imagine. Wasn't she always instructing people? Giving the kids a little smack on the bottom? Helping the medicine go down with a spoonful of sugar? That's me. You can't believe the propaganda against me. I am closer to Julie Andrews than Pol Pot. Really. The guards should be playing "Do-Re-Mi" in the background. Look—look, my friends. Can't we just say I am guilty of something and move on? Who goes through life without being guilty of something? I am just a good guy with bad press. My people genuinely applauded me for a long time. *This* should have been my logo:

(He goes to the projector and draws a happy face.)

Instead of my portraits everywhere this should have been what they saw.

(He will continue to draw two or three more happy faces.)

If I ever get back into power I will put these up instead. I will personally see to everyone's happiness. I'll have my police knocking on every door to ask if people are happy. And if not, why not. The pursuit of happiness,

THE TYRANT 49

like you. I will hunt it down till everyone has a piece of it.

But instead of doing that, you drag me here like a modern day Cleopatra and parade me. How like an empire you behave—as much as you like to think you're not. So like you to get all cozy with strong leaders and then dump them. Don't *you* have any morals? Do you even *know* what's being done in your name? To this day? My God, the privilege of being you. Having the power to outsource your darkest deeds so you don't have to look in the abyss. *We do it for you and then get attacked for doing it. All so you can continue your pursuit of happiness. And amusing yourselves to death while we get bent over.* Well fuck you too!

(A warning sound and red light come on for a couple of beats.)

Oh shut up! I am the President of a country! You think you can step on me like shit? *You* brought me down! Not my people!

(The door swings open. He turns to see it.)

Ah. At last. Now watch. They will take me out and beat me. You will see how they treat me here. I will not go quietly! Come in and show your true face! Show them how you treat your prisoners here….Well come on. Show your faces to these people.

(No one comes.)

These guards. Like thugs everywhere. No heart. No mind even.

(American accent.)

"Just doing my job."

(Back to regular accent.)

Your efficiency is inhuman! At least we put heart into our punishing. You? Like robots. All tick-tock and no heart. Come in here, damn you! Let them see how you treat a leader who inspired a nation!

(He goes to the door to look out, if he hasn't done so already.)

Do you see the mind games they play? You see how they want to drive me mad first? Turn my brain into the tapioca pudding they serve me, *if* I'm good....

Oh I see. I am to return to my cell on my own. Like a dog they are trying to train me. Sit. Stand. Eat. Do you see? A dog!

I demand an escort back to my cell!

(The lights will start dimming. Slight beat.)

Was I not honest enough? Did I not confess to everything? It is *you* who is not being honest with them.

I see…I see…from now on it is to be this way. I was warned it would come to this. All lights and sounds. And commands. No contact. I am to be starved of human contact. Good; good. Take a man who lives off the love and respect of a people and deny him even a hello. You are so very good at this. How inspiring. How like amateurs we were.

(To the audience)

Do you see how it works? …Do you?…

(Sincerely appealing to his audience.)

I was your man…. You don't want to get rid of me. Some people's demands should never be given in to. My people do not have the character for freedom. They are on a course they do not understand. They'll ruin everything. And their ruin will come to your shores. It will come to your shores!

(As the lights dim further, a single shaft of light coming through the door will illuminate the stage. To the prison staff:)

You are just going to shut the lights on me?

(Slight beat)

Cleopatra was so smart. You can not stick around when the end comes. When the end has come for you, you should not be there to witness it. The disrespect — is intolerable.

(Slight beat. To the audience. Gathering his dignity)

I hope you have been sufficiently entertained by this spectacle. You, on the other hand, have been a very disappointing audience.

(He goes to the door.)

Too late you will understand my place in your lives. Too late.

But you can not rob me of my memories. I know my accomplishments. No one can enter my head and imprison me there. I am free where it counts. It is you, your lives, what you do not understand about how you are able to have this life you live. You are the ones locked up.

(He steps out into the hallway.)

In here.

(Taps his head)

In here is where it counts. In here…I will always be President. President for life.

(From the hallway, he looks out at the audience. The last light goes out. Blackout)

END OF PLAY

THE BIRDS FLEW IN

THE BIRDS FLEW IN was first Performed at Golden Thread Productions' ReOrient Festival in 2012 *(San Francisco)*. The cast and creative contributor were:

NADIA .... Nora El Samahy
Director .... Evren Odcikin

THE BIRDS FLEW IN was next performed at On The Board's 12 Minutes Max series in 2013 *(Seattle)*. The cast and creative contributor were:

NADIA .... Gin Hammond
Director .... Sean Ryan

THE BIRDS FLEW IN was also performed at West of Lenin's "Three Americans: Voices of Hope" in 2017 *(Seattle)*. The cast and creative contributor were:

NADIA .... Annette Toutonghi
Director .... Anita Montgomery

CHARACTER

Nadia, *anywhere from late 30s to late 50s*

(A woman sits alone, dressed for a funeral. There are several chairs around the stage. A jacket is draped over one chair.)

(Note to actor: the speech is delivered without self-pity, melancholy or languor. There is a matter-of-factness to her approach that masks the overwhelming emotions that are tearing her apart. Though, yes, there are places where the emotions break through. This is a woman who is trying to keep it together, even as these emotions are at play. Perhaps what does peek through more than anything is anger. Not too much. She's trying to put a lid on everything's that's too much.)

NADIA: His not being here will become a problem as the weeks pass. His absence. There is an absence now….

Before this, my life summed up in his. Summed up in waking up and knowing he was there. What my life added up to. And now—there is this cutting out. The heart, stomped on. Strange how literal that feels. There are body parts now. His. Mine. I think I will stop this.

Now that the guests have gone. The well-wishers. The mourners. His bastard friends who egged him on. "I'm so sorry", they say. Leaning in, their breaths. "I'm so sorry for your loss." The little shits. They'll go home and fuck tonight. Mourn mourn, then off to rut. Their useless seeds getting passed on. And mine….

(…)

So I'm sitting here and this woman says, "You should be proud. Your son made the ultimate sacrifice". And

I looked at her, her face—the concern that cost her nothing, and I wanted to peel off her pretend grief and spit it back like it was really spit.

(A moment as she recalls a memory; the memory.)

So we were talking, my son and I, he'd come home and he—. Wait.

(She puts her hand near her mouth.)

Am I saying this out loud? —Testing. —No air. I must be thinking this.

(...)

So Sami comes home and he says. "Mom, I know you're not going to like this." That's how he begins; and he's serious. But he's smiling because he knows he's going to piss me off. So he's trying to lighten it up. Because he knows that this might like, you know, kill me. And it has. Not into my grave, but zombie-like now. Talking to you, to no one. Just hearing my voice ramble on like maggots pouring out of some carcass. —I will talk like this now forever. Even when enough grief has passed, a part of me will always be quietly mumbling to myself about you. Did you think of me you selfish little shit? Didn't you think I might die many times more than you ever could. *My* body suffers first. *I* get sacrificed. You enlist *me*. *I* take the bullet, *my* head bursts. *Did you ever stop to think*?

(Steps out of the stream for a moment. Then:)

I thought I had to be tough. Tell you not to cry when you wanted to. Don't play with dolls, no, play with this pretend gun. This is what fathers do, after your father died. This is how you grow up to be a man. God forbid he should grow up to be a sissy. I don't know what's wrong with being a sissy but we can't have him turn out to be one.

(...)

THE BIRDS FLEW IN

So he comes home and says he wants to join the army. "Ha", I say. I'm eating something, toast. Staring at this bird outside our window, wondering if she'll take the crumb.

"I'm serious", he says.

And I look at him now. To read his face; to see signs of a joke. And I think: he's gotten good at this. He's got that deadpan look down. And I look at him for real now, because the look in his eyes seem to be saying, "I'm not joking".

(A moment as she seems to stare back at the memory.)

And for a moment he's six years old again — about to do some dangerous thing. And mommy needs to lecture him about how he should never think to do such a thing. But there he is, all eighteen years of him, daring me to try that mommy thing again, as if dropping a couple of testicles now entitles him to act stupidly. I should have given him dolls to play with. Made him wear pink. What a silly thing to want your boy to be "a man". Most of the men I've met in my life haven't been very bright. The more manly a man is the less there is to play with up here.

(Taps her head)

The sissies are the clever ones. I should have brought him up to be a sissy. —So I say the first mommy thing that comes to me. "Don't be silly."

And he walks away.

And the air rushes out of the room.

And the bird hops into the kitchen and flies around. Later, when I tell my friend about this, she says that was bad luck. —A bird flying into your house is bad luck, apparently. But I invited the bird in with the crumb, I say, doesn't that make a difference? Apparently not. In the book of good luck and bad, having a bird flying inside your house is bad. It's just bad. —I argue with her, as if she's Luck's ambassador. As if I could go back and negotiate with the gods of good luck and bad and have them rethink the outcome.

(To the gods)

"I invited the bird in", I would tell these gods, *"isn't that a mitigating factor?"*

(Hold a moment as if waiting for the reply, then:)

Later that night I sit beside him on his bed.

Wrong move, again. He bolts up into a sitting position and I get off the bed like we've both been electrocuted. Then the third mistake, I say: "Is this about proving you're a man?"

(...)

I didn't mean for it to sound condescending. I really didn't. I see he's about to be swallowed up whole by all those man things that are supposed to make you stand tall, and I don't know the argument for that. How are you supposed to stop a boy from becoming the thing you taught him to be? I say, *"We left our country to get you out of war. And now you want to run into one? Do you know how much we lost? The sacrifices to bring you to this country? Your father never recovered"*.

"And now I want to give back", he says. "I want to give back to the country that accepted us, that has given me so much." Oh, God, you little shit. You're going to spit some civics course back in my face? And turn every common sense thing I have to say into something cowardly sounding? You're going to actually drag in some fucking rhetoric spouted by every two-bit politician and wave the flag. "I'm an American, mom", he says. Or weren't you aware of that while raising me here."

THE BIRDS FLEW IN

I say, "We don't do countries. We do family. You and me, we do survival. Because where we come from, that's what you do. We *know* governments. Governments eat people. Just because this one here has a smiley face on it doesn't mean it won't swallow you too".

He says: "I hope I never get to be as cynical as you. And if you try and argue me out of this you'll be telling me to stop being all the things you taught me to be. And I won't let you do that".

(Staring back at the memory, as she continues to live in the memory.)

The next thing he does is put on his robe. Over his shorts. As if I am now a stranger to his body. As if that robe is the curtain being pulled down on the boy I knew and now this was the man I had to deal with.

"Do you know what they say about us?" he says. "The crap that's spewed in my face because of where we come from? What they call us because of that?"

"So what?" I scream. "Let them talk! They're free to be as stupid as they want to be in this country! And we're just as free to ignore them." —I'm shouting. As if I'm addressing the people who said these things to my son. And then from his mouth he repeats "I'm an American". As if that declaration is the answer to all my questions. This complete non sequitur. This whole conversation feels like it's coming out of nowhere. Like I'm staring at my boy who's now trapped in some parallel universe where you have to make these grand proclamations about who you are just to breathe. And he finishes his declaration with, "And nobody's going to take that away from me".

(…)

And at that moment, all the birds in the world are flying into our apartment.

(Remembers the moment, then:)

Flap, flap.

(…)

The next morning I forbid him to go. But he says he's already signed the contract. There's a brief period of hysteria. I plead with him. I weep at one point. And then he leaves.

Later I get a few emails when he's over there. A few phone calls. We talk about nothing. Which is such an art. Talking about nothing when we both have the world to say to each other. When everything I have to say to him is like some booby trap inside of me, which we both have to avoid.

And then the two soldiers who knock on my door…. The funeral…. The well-wishers. The very people who may have questioned how American he was, sitting here, paying their respects to me, his mother…. The man who sat here says to me, "You may have lost a son, but you have a hero now. And heroes are never forgotten". …Do you have *any* contact with any living thing that you think that would console me?

(Beat. She removes the jacket from the chair next to her revealing an American flag that's been folded into the tricornered shape common at military funerals. She picks it up and places it on her lap. Looks at it, then:)

Satisfied now?

(Another moment as she stares at the flag, then:)

But the thing that keeps me awake….

What keeps me awake. Is maybe I didn't try hard enough. To find the right argument. To persuade you from going…. Because you see, somewhere in some horrible little corner — I *was* proud. In spite of my anger. I was proud…. That's the horrible thing that flew in that day. In all its glorious feathers…my pride…. You had grown up to be a man after all…. I had done my job.

(Slow fade to black)

END OF PLAY

THE MONOLOGIST SUFFERS HER MONOLOGUE

THE MONOLOGIST SUFFERS HER MONOLOGUE
First performed at Golden Thread Productions' ReOrient Festival in San Francisco in 2008. The cast and creative contributor were:

HODA..Sara Razavi

Director... Arlene Hood

CHARACTER

HODA, *any age*

(*Stage could be bare. Or perhaps* HODA*'s sitting on a stool.*)

HODA: Among the drama of nations,

if nations were types of dramas,

Palestine would be a monologue.

A lone voice yapping away like some animal separated from the herd (to, er, hook another image to the monologue for a second), caught in a trap, and—you hear it in the distance, hear its wails, and—you wish it well…and you wish it would stop—frankly. You wish whatever pain it was in would end. Mainly so you could get on with your day. Which you're having a hard enough time trying to get through as it is. And when you know you can't, when you know it won't shut up or go away, you begin to, well—you tune it out. You tune out this painful monologue. You start to say—to hell with it. It is what it is. Perhaps it has always been this way. Perhaps it was born to be an example of something or other to appreciate what you have and take for granted: a country. With borders. A place you can hurry back to when the world around you is too much, too unwelcoming. A flag you can stick on your head like those toy propeller blades stuck on hats that kids used to wear, and that look so silly, much like flags do, actually, look silly; really, the whole concept. But with a flag you can make believe you're moving about some imagined territory that's yours, with its own air space and edges; that welcomes you and wants you; and even though this imagined place is an illusion, it's one you all agree on, so everyone can live and play in their own spot.

So, yes:

among nations, Palestine is a monologue. Is living a monologue. And you see, when people talk to you, the Palestinian, when people ask about it, about this annoying wail that seeps through their waking day now and again, this on-going groan that never seems to end, and you, the Palestinian, explain,

you—

you become this monologue. Because really, the person is probably not engaging you in a one-on-one sit down, with the intention of forming a bond of any kind, (I mean, maybe, but not essentially) no, the question of Palestine, the questions about Palestine places you, the mouthpiece of — the accidental representative of this still unacknowledged place, places you

in that—

dreadful explanation mode where you—though your lips are moving, your mouth actually is open in this rictus of—

(She opens her mouth wide.)

—rictus of deep angst where you find yourself once again having to prove to seemingly intelligent people the equivalent of the world is round, or, in this case, that you exist. I'm here. I'm—I'm talking. I'm talking to you. And the question, you see, is directed at that, essentially, when you break it down, when you sort it out and trace the genealogy behind every question, you come down to that:

do you have a right to all the perks that come with a person who exists? And a person only really exists when they can lay claim to something as basic as a—as a country. It's all right being a free spirit slash citizen of

THE MONOLOGIST SUFFERS HER MONOLOGUE

the world, but first you need to have a place that claims you as its own before you can go off gallivanting about without need of addressing that faint sense that you're not quite, um, legitimate. And if you can't do that—if you can't have a free and easy dialogue with others without all those issues hanging in the air, then you're...stuck in a monologue.

And what is more troubling, you see,

as you become this never-ending monologue,

you, the monologist, basically suffer the risk of becoming your own echo chamber. So that essential, life-affirming words like "fairness" and "justice", and let's throw in "truth", they lose all semblance of reality. So that you may end up going a little loopy without any verifiable bridges that can lead you out—outside of yourself.

Okay: wait: let me back up.

We all suffer from talking to ourselves too much. Never mind Palestine for the moment. It's a shame we can't do more with our brain than subject it to the nonsensical stuff that overwhelms us every day. It's bad enough struggling to say, "Hi, can I draw your attention to this little boot that's on our neck", but simply being human is teeth-gnashing all by itself. And there's something to be said for those—I have to say—chatter-ceasing drugs like Zoloft and Prozac. Speaking of which—and, really, I don't want to alarm you, but let me just say this: I'm not sure there's a point to all this.

This might have a point. I'm not ruling that out. But I just want to apologize ahead of time in case.

Especially since I have a personal distaste for monologues. Or mono dramas. Or solo performances.

I hate them, to be honest.

I detest monologues. And those who practice them. Subjecting an audience who could be at home watching T V, or making love with their partner, or enjoying a home-cooked meal, are instead listening to someone yammer away about something that's really not half as important as the person thinks it is. I mean who do these people think they are?

Standing in front of an audience for a chunk of time, bitching about some personal experience or other, and I'm like, no: your life is not that interesting. I don't want to know why someone dumped you, or what happened when you went home for thanksgiving. If I want to listen to someone bitch for an hour I'll listen to myself yap, and God knows I make an honest enough effort not to encourage my own tendencies; which are huge, as I've been saying, huge, I'm consumed by my need to talk. So why should I listen to you bitch and moan when I can barely tolerate it in myself?

Monologues are just bastards.

They really are. They are the bastard children of drama.

Runts.

Stateless.

Very much like refugees, and we know how monotone they can be, always in open-mouth mode and needy ("I'm suffering, I'm bleeding, I'm dying"). No. No, monologues are really failures of the imagination to imagine relationships outside of the speaker's own little world.

A stand-up routine of sorts without the benefit of laughs (usually). And there's usually this flop-sweat hanging over the monologist if he or she can't keep one step ahead of collapsing in on herself, more than she already has. Because the weight, the only weight the monologist seems able to bear is the weight of her own words because everything else feels like a betrayal.

An abandonment.

And in this, the monologist is—well…

very much like Palestine…if you will.

So full of her own necessity and presence and at the same time, nursing this sense of feeling—abandoned. So full of herself *because* of this feeling of being abandoned. Like she should have been cast in *something*, damn it. Signed up with the cast list of other nations.

And instead of being a good little actor and trying again later she has the audacity to strike out on her own because she has a lot to say and will not be shut up.

So. Anyway. Yes:

no full-fledged drama tonight.

Just me.

And I'm not enough of a drama queen to make up for it.

And as I said, this is really all by way of stating this, er, this basic idea which is—basically a very long aside (sorry),

but which is,

"In the drama of nations Palestine is a monologue." With the obvious or not so obvious follow up that Palestine, when all is said and done, over and above being a country that has yet to be acknowledged, officially, and celebrated, and allowed to participate on the world stage, etc., that Palestine, really, is,

it becomes…a state of mind.

Which can affect us all.

Regardless of whether you are or aren't Palestinian. That is…

should you ever find yourself alone, among a group of strangers; and you aren't able to make a connection, try as you might, please take note that at that moment you are in fact an honorary member of a state that currently has no solid borders. You can just say to yourself, at that point, as you fail to get through and people look at you like you're barfing up something that really should be left alone, you can just say, "Gee: I guess I'm in a Palestine State of Mind". This is how it must feel. Not quite a member. Or: dismembered. With a lot of reassembling going on even as you try to take apart the wrong ideas they have of you. This Frankenstein they have cobbled together in place of you, to *place* you, and which waddles about their imagination even as you stand there full in their face and speaking. Only to yourself as it turns out. And you know the torch-bearing mob and the end credits and the climactic music are never far behind. Yes, at that point, I'd have to say…welcome to my country.

(Slight beat. Blackout)

END OF PLAY

SO UNLIKE ME

SO UNLIKE ME was performed as part of VIA's "Solo Shorts" in Seattle in 2003. The cast and creative contributor were:

BARBARA .... Clare Aronow
Director .... Sean Ryan

CHARACTER

BARBARA, *from 40s to 60s*

(Two chairs, a desk. On the desk: paper, pen and a phone. A T V set with its back to the audience flickers on mute. BARBARA, a woman in her 40s or older, may start off either seated or standing.)

BARBARA: The thing is…

The disturbing thing—the thing that is most unsettling…in the midst of everything else that is unsettling now is how…I'm beginning to alter my views on certain matters. In spite of my firm beliefs in resolving things in a peaceful way. I still believe that, of course. I have to. We have to. I'm so glad to hear you're still out there protesting, doing your part. We must keep going regardless. No matter how futile it seems. Or pathetic our little signs seem to be against this terrific might. Do you continue to believe that, by the way?

(Slight beat)

I should have got back to you sooner, I'm sorry. I've hardly spoken to anyone this past week. I want to say so much to you. And I will. I'll pick up the phone in a moment and talk to you. But I need to rehearse it in my mind first to be absolutely clear about what I want to say. Are you changing your opinion on anything, now that we seem to have been swept aside?

(Slight beat)

I often wonder what is going on in the minds of the people I am closest to in this struggle. It's so odd feeling like strangers in the midst of all this passion.

Though I suppose we're united in that. I think that's what's so life-affirming about what we did. We're still doing. And we can't lose that. We mustn't allow ourselves to be pushed back into our little worlds, where we end up shouting at the T V, or muttering under our breath and feeling like we can't do anything. Feeling like spectators. The worst thing of all that: being made a spectator to this blood sport, and I won't allow myself to become that. I won't have them turn this into a movie for us, where we're supposed to just stare ahead and watch whatever they parade before us. This nauseating little drama they've cooked up is ours. We're in it. And it's for us to change. My conscience has not been put to sleep. I will not stare dumbly ahead, and I will not allow this.

(Slight beat)

I really should have got back to you. You ask me how I'm feeling. Not well. I have in fact been talking to myself. In a productive way I hope. I think there's a difference between talking to yourself and muttering under your breath. I think being aware of what one is saying—articulating it in round sounds so that the whole room hears you is much more healthy than the shuffling around of words in your mouth. And I think to do that you have to be very clear about what you mean. And I'm not. I am clear about needing to get to that point, because not having it sorted out for myself is driving me a little nutty. And the nuttier I get the less able I am to sort things out.

(Slight beat)

What am I trying to say to you?

(She goes over to the desk, picks up the pen, looks at the sheet of paper. Then puts them both down.)

I went out last night….I went out…finally.

SO UNLIKE ME

I'd had enough of everything, most of all myself, and decided a walk would be just the thing. So—I went out.

And walked, aimlessly. Thinking about a conversation I'd had with Jillian. You've never met my daughter, but she's a pretty spunky egg. And she was telling me how depressed she was about everything and how useless she felt. And I gave her the speech about speaking one's mind regardless, and resisting, and the untapped powers of the spirit, etcetera. And how peace is not some cry-baby that wails and wails until something comes along and puts it back to sleep, but an active force. A grown-up, adult thing that more people needed to take seriously. And so on. And I hung up. And felt sick. And went for a walk and thought about what I'd said, and wondered why I was feeling like an utter fraud when my progress was blocked by this… this police car that had been parked right across the sidewalk. Just right across it, completely blocking all pedestrian traffic. You had to walk around it and out on the street. There were no other police cars or anything to suggest an emergency, or something dire going on. Most of the lights in the houses were out. It was very quiet. The police person was probably visiting his girlfriend or something, and had just casually parked his imposing little vehicle like that because he could. Because he had the authority. And I stopped in front of it…and fumed. I took a moment to try to be understanding, after all, it could have been an emergency.

Then walked around it…

Muttering under my breath…

I got back on the sidewalk. Continued walking… saw this hefty rock in someone's garden, picked it up, walked back to the police car and hurled it at the windshield. —And saw it shatter into that awful spider pattern....

I stood there for a moment. Telling myself, okay. I wasn't expecting that. I hadn't planned on doing *that*. But now that I have, here I am, and I'm ready to face the consequences. I will get arrested and I will tell the judge why I had done such a thing. Even though I wasn't exactly sure why I had done it. I was actually quite breathless looking at it. Astonished. I couldn't believe it. Then I wanted to stay so I could tell the cop, "Look: look at what I've done. Isn't that amazing? Could you ever imagine such a thing. From me. I've just broken your windshield. With that rock".

And I was in such a state, I actually imagined the cop might say, "Wow. That is amazing. You did that?" "Yes, I did". And we would both marvel at what I'd done. Then he would smile, shake his head in consternation, get in his car, wish me a good night and drive away.

(Slight beat)

Then I came to my senses, sort of. Realized I didn't want to get arrested. Started backing up, turned around and gunned it down the street. I mean really flew. All the while thinking, "I'm a fleeing felon, I'm a fleeing felon". Over and over until the words made no sense and I started to giggle because by the time I reached my home I was down to "I'm a feeling melon; I'm a famous flan; I'm a favorite flimflam". I was definitely losing it.

I came home. Utterly breathless. Felt just as breathless after I had calmed my body down. I locked the door behind me. And—stood in this room, in various poses of shock. My mouth open for long stretches of time. Like a caricature of someone with their mouth open.

I caught myself in the mirror at one point and I really did look like a character in a Kabuki play.

I rushed to the window to see if I had been followed, and ducked in case I had. I think I crawled to the couch to hide behind at one point. Then I ate a tub of ice-cream for some reason. Then threw up. And passed out. But, John—the thing is—the somewhat disturbing thing to me is—this morning, when I recalled everything—when I remembered, I was…thrilled.

After that initial, "Oh-my-god" moment when I woke up. But too soon after that I felt…great. It was like I'd just had—great sex. You know, that—warm feeling when your whole body feels like it's gotten an answer to something that's been nagging at it for a while. It was like what I had done had been absolutely on the mark. And obviously — I mean obviously it wasn't. Because it was so wrong. I felt great, but felt awful for feeling so satisfied. I mean you can't have people going round lugging rocks at cop cars. You just can't. It's bad all the way around and sets a terrible example. And I know I ought to feel ashamed and I'm sure I will, eventually, but, John, I had no idea behavior of this sort was this much…fun. —I mean…

What a revelation….

Don't get me wrong: it's not as if I've been little Ms Peace-Maker all my life. I've had my share of violent fits. Just last week at the rally I wanted to wring Angela's neck for hogging the microphone and saying the stupidest things. I'm sorry if I seem too critical, but I think there was a collective groan in the audience when she started praying for all the domestic pets that might get caught in the crossfire. What was she doing talking about the cats and dogs of the "other side"? For a good fifteen minutes. You could tell the people were racking their brains wondering if they should be feeling guilty for not feeling anything on this issue, or if they were right in thinking the speaker was an idiot. I had a lot of violent thoughts that day.

But I didn't act any of them out. Thank God we have this circuit breaker called a conscience that forbids us from acting out our awful impulses. What is troubling to me is twenty-four hours later my conscience is dancing a merry jig....

Only...if I am troubled it can't be my conscience dancing a merry jig, can it. Though I can't say I'm feeling that troubled, to be honest, which is worrying. But that worry isn't really my conscience acting up either as it is me feeling queasy for not feeling as guilty as I should feel. John:

What if....

What if we haven't fully understood the nature of the thing we're so appalled by. What if...we're actually clueless about the force we're so against. What if its true nature has so escaped us that when we say "*non*violence" our emphasis on the "non" ends up acting as a negative, as a paralyzing force, because we refuse to own up to its deep appeal to us. What if violence actually has some relation to the good in us and brings about better things.

Okay. Okay.

Bear with me. I'm trying to put this together myself.

In fact I'll probably just write this all down rather than call you. And please be assured I am not changing philosophies. I am not about to drop nonviolence and become an armed commando. Not with my lack of physical coordination. And certainly not because of last night. I'm well aware that my little bump of enthusiasm was from the rush of doing something terribly naughty. And an inarticulate "fuck you" screamed at an unreasonable pitch is sometimes the most articulate and reasonable thing you can do. I would suggest you try it if it wasn't so insane. I mean poor, that poor policeman, discovering that. But John. Yes, I understand the nature of that thrill, but I think there's a reason violence remains so—ever present.

We're…we're really sick puppies, John. I'm not sure we own up to just how much shit we're dealing with. And it's sloshing around in us even as we chant "world peace". And yes, we do nonviolence because we understand just how violent we can get and work hard to appeal to the best in us, the higher stuff. In the meantime, the lower stuff stays where it is and ten thousand years later, after some pretty amazing expressions of the human spirit, we're acting more like beasts than the beasts we were to begin with. From which we've supposedly evolved. I mean look at us. Look at us.

But—

what I'm getting to.

What I'm trying to understand for myself.

Yes: there's that.

But mingled with that. There's this enormous power that comes with being—fucked up. That may be just frustration and insecurity needing an out, or anger at not having the world conform the way you want it to but, also, I think—it may be just what is needed. A vomiting of something — deeply necessary, that needs to have its day. In all its rawness, and rudeness, for the chaos it unleashes. *Because* of the chaos it unleashes. I mean I'm trying to understand its appeal so we don't always come off looking so lame. At least in war there's this sense of adventure. In peace, what? There's no adventure in peace. It doesn't take you anywhere, or test your manhood, or whatever. It's static. And comes with the same tired messages: "be nice", "live in harmony", "love thy neighbor", blah blah blah. It's not very sexy, is it. Maybe if we were gurus living on some ethereal plane where we could tap into this great whatever it'd be different. But we're not. We're saps knee deep in mud trying to get by, and what we offer isn't—it doesn't give enough of us the "umph" we need to last beyond our protests. And in war, there's "umph" to spare.

And I'm fed up of feeling powerless, John. I'm—fed up.

Nothing…nothing we've done so far has made the slightest dent in anything. And being told that you never know what influence you may be having or this one-person-at-a-time thing isn't good enough. And frankly—I don't think speaking out does anything. I don't think our speaking up has made the slightest bit of difference. We make such a big deal about it but what has it actually done?

When we come together and raise our voices. And speak as one. And so on. All those expressions we use to comfort ourselves into believing we're doing something, when we're not, are we, if we're being honest. We're not. And the depressing thing is, I don't think this approach has ever had the effect we think it's had. Even those glorious examples in the past that we always point to of what can happen when people assemble to give voice to something. That was never—peaceful assembly was never a deciding factor. When you look at it, historically. When you examine the forces that finally moved things in the right direction. It always required a little more. And I'm not talking about civil disobedience here.

(Slight beat)

SO UNLIKE ME

I know what I'm saying would lead to something I could never support. I would never go down that road.

But I have to tell you…in my head…

I have a picture now of what might lead someone to do some—terrible thing….Behave in a way that would make everyone stop shopping for a second and pay attention. Engage in an act that is not healing. Or good; that is bad, in every way, but that is very, very necessary. I have that glimpse now. I do have that understanding. Me, who could never imagine wrapping my mind around such things; or willfully setting out to hurt or do harm, I'm there. In my head. I am hurting the thing that belittles my concerns. I am breaking its bones. I am crushing it, John. I am getting through. I am not powerless anymore. I am not—*powerless*.

(*Beat*)

And that is why we keep on doing what we're doing. Right?…

Stop those feelings from getting together and—justifying each other and coming up with a plan. A nasty plan. Even if our approach to stopping that seems to be as effective as someone talking to themselves in a room. Or worse, to each other in our case, in one endless spiraling echo—back and forth, back and forth; giving each other support for all our pathetic little concerns which might as well be as if we were each alone talking to an empty room. Or muttering under our breath at the T V. Or shouting at it. —Or shouting at it.

(*Beat*)

Yes.

Yes.

So there you are.

(Slight beat)

It's normal, of course. I know that.

Having doubts. Reassessing. It's healthy. —Thank God I haven't stopped meditating. It has kept me really grounded.

(Slight beat)

Yes.

So there you are.

(She goes to her desk, picks up her pen.)

We'll be fine.

(Slight beat)

We'll be fine.

(Her pen hovers over the page, then she writes.)

Call me when you get this letter.

I'll have sorted things out I'm sure by the time you get this, and then we can set up another meeting.

I'll be back with the program, I promise. My apologies to everyone for being absent.

I love you. We're doing good work. I know we are. These are just…

(She hesitates. Then crosses out what she'd started to write.)

Love, Barbara.

(She signs her name. She puts the letter in an envelope. Picks up the pen to address it. Hesitates. Then tears up the envelope/letter.)

(She puts on her coat. She picks up the pieces of the envelope/letter and stuffs them into her coat pocket. She picks up the remote and stands in front of the T V.)

(She stares at the T V for a moment before turning up the volume. We hear a montage of various news reports.)

(The sounds begin to overlap as the volume increases.)

(The lights begin to fade, leaving only the light from the T V flickering, almost in a strobe-like effect. She puts the remote down, leaving the T V blaring. She exits. The loud sound of the door slamming signals the blackout.)

END OF PLAY

THE SNIPER

THE SNIPER was first performed at Golden Thread Productions' ReOrient Festival in San Francisco in 2005. The cast and creative contributor were:

JOHN .... William Todd Tessler
Director .... Hal Gelb

CHARACTER

JOHN, *anywhere from 30s to 40s*

(*A living room.* JOHN *enters talking into a recording device. He carries a bag of chips, a soda.*)

JOHN: Babs? Call me. Where are you? Stop playing Garbo? Depression is optional. All is not lost.

Drugs are available.

Just because you think the world is going to hell doesn't mean there isn't a drug out there that can make you feel good about things.

(*Turns off recording device. Switches it back on*)

Not that I'm suggesting a pharmaceutical approach to war and world depravity. But I think your whole—toxin-free approach completely overlooks the value of a good pill. Pop one. You don't have to suffer while working to make the world a better place. Atrocities may be taking place but why fret about them? If there's a drug out there that can make you smile while reading the latest Amnesty report, take it. It will lift your spirits up. I'll pop one with you.

I needed one yesterday at the meeting you so cleverly avoided.

Kevin spoke. Yes. Yes, he did. And because he bored everyone into a stupor, nobody had their wits about them to cut him off. He just blathered on until Daniels groaned, just groaned, and whispered loud enough for everyone to hear that he was going to kill himself.

It's generally unhelpful to provoke that feeling in a pep talk meant to rally the troops. When your motivational speaker implants suicidal thoughts in your core activists: not good.

And what was the topic of this speech? you ask. "How To Say No To Empire and Remain a Patriot." He actually ended up making Empire sound good. Like it would be a breath of fresh air compared to him. Another big no-no: don't make the other side seem more attractive than your side.

Anyway. You're not allowed to miss the next one. Some things we should suffer together, in the absence of pills.

Omar's coming round. He'll pick up this tape and drop it off with the minutes of the meeting. We know you're alive because you picked up the last envelope. Otherwise we would have called the police on you. Where are you? Answer your emails. So we didn't succeed in anything we set out to do, so what? Snap out of it. It's besides the point if we're a useless bunch who've devoted our lives to engaging in activities that have little impact.

I'm telling you, Babs, pills. We need to seriously look into them.

(He punches numbers into his cell-phone.)

Trying you one more time — on the off-chance you've forgotten you're not answering your phone. It's kind of stupid resorting to taped messages when there're simpler ways to communicate….

(He listens.)

Pick up, pick up….

(He slumps, or performs some physical action to indicate he's gotten her voice mail. Then, he holds the cell-phone and recorder like they're dolls.)

THE SNIPER

"Hello taped message. May I introduce you to my taped message." "No, leave your message and I'll get back to you." "Can't I just talk to you now?" "No you can't. The world's a mess and I've decided to check out." "Well that's a bit cowardly don't you think?" "Mind your own business and fuck off." "'Fuck off', you say? I bet you're turning into a conservative crank even as we speak." "Well better a conservative crank than a puny peacenik like you." "Yeah, well eat my peacenik you turncoat."

(Into the recorder)

These—

(Remembers he's still on the line, he switches to the cellphone.)

These are the conversations I'm reduced to.

Don't dump us. Please? I can't do group hugs without you. I need one person in there who uses deodorant. Plus I have to tell you what happened at the party you missed. It was very weird, and — very sexual. Weird, and…just very strange. People felt the need to be nude. And express themselves through body parts normally reserved for loved ones. It was kind of like Vagina Monologues meets Karl Marx with a lot of veganism thrown in. You'll have to call me back if you want the full story. Animals were involved. In spite of the vegans. Okay, bye.

(Hangs up. Then, into the recorder)

You may have to splice these two messages together for the phone message to make sense. I'm not joking about the sex. They introduced new condoms made from recycled army surplus parachutes. It's the new campaign from the "Swords into Plowshares" outfit. Heck of a party. Who knew activists could party that hard. Call if you want more info.

(Turns off the recorder. He takes a drink from his soda. He looks at his watch. If he hasn't already opened the bag of chips, he does so now and eats. A couple of beats pass as he does this. Then he picks up the recorder.)

Okay, so this is what happened. I started this so I could tell you about what happened on Saturday. So I'm at the party, Joan's party, which was more of a gathering really, and I'm one of the first ones there. And she introduces me to this guy. And let me just say I may have overstated the part about the sex. As bait. To get you to call me. There was sex in a—quasi theoretical sort of way but, just not a lot of body contact to go with it. Mostly as chatter. Anyway. —Sorry. This is really about a small realization I had at a pretty dull party. So Joan introduces me to this guy. And you know how she is, she gives these long intros to give the people she's introducing a lot to talk about, and she starts with me, says, this is John, peace activist, blah blah blah, former C E O of a company, recently sold to fight various progressive causes. Anti-war this and that. Throws in my sexual orientation, like she knows, but doesn't, and that I'm single.

And then she turns to the other guy and says: this is Mark. Mark, she says, is a former army person. He received a medal for something in the last war and now is a security guard for the company that ships night vision goggles to the army. Also single, not sure about his sexual orientation, but I believe he's a Baptist. And then adds that Mark trained as a sniper while serving.

Then she leaves to check on dinner.

And the introduction was such that I think we both thought she was trying to set us up as a couple. You know Joan, matchmaker that she is. She thinks the world's problems could be solved if everyone was fucking all the time. Which I agree with essentially, but she continues to believe I'm gay for some reason. Anyway. So the first thing Mark says, by way of clearing the air is: "I'm straight".

And that, Babs...that...was the only thing that ticked me off about that guy for the entire evening. Almost the entire evening. That he needed to clear that up. Which is fine, I guess. It wasn't a big deal—that he wanted to make that clear to ward off unwanted advances, but...

I found myself...

not taking issue with anything else about this guy.

And you may ask, why should you? It's a party. He's a nice guy, which he was. This wasn't a rally or political meeting, nobody had to bat around agendas. People aren't—we aren't walking policy statements.

You can have a conversation with someone engaged in activities you don't agree with and still have fun. Especially if his beliefs and activities might be two different things. And that's what I assumed. That's what we all assumed when others came. That here was another luckless soul who—through—economic necessity had been forced into this route: army, war. Security guard for war profiteers because jobs are hard to find, etc. I don't think any of us thought that he might enjoy what he was doing, or had done. We all gave him the benefit of the doubt. In fact there wasn't much doubt. There was barely any questioning.

I'm not explaining this right. You're going to hear this and wonder what I'm—what my problem with this was.

It's why I wish you were here so we could talk about it.

I'd actually like to bring this up in the next meeting. I think it *should* be brought up in the next meeting. I don't think it's a small realization at all. I think what happened at that party kind of...

typifies a problem we're having and I think is what makes us so....

Because we seem to be so...stuck in this — in these weird contradictions. Because what happened at this party, you see, what I found myself doing was...

I felt very protective of this guy. I felt the need to be nice, and say the right things; and reverse any expectations he might have of *me*. And I think he felt the same way. That he wasn't going to let a small matter of philosophical differences stand in the way of a polite conversation. We aren't *only* the sum total of our beliefs and actions. Though what's left after that I don't know. Anyway. —Shit.

(He switches off the recorder. To himself)

What do you want to say, John?

What?

Summarize. Be succinct.

(Into the recorder)

I think I got so upset later on because I realized the problem lay with me.

For having been so...exceptionally civil. I've sometimes thought the problem with my upbringing is that I was taught civility and politeness are the most important things in any encounter.

And of course they should be. You *want* civility when bringing together a group of people with different opinions. It helps keep those thoughts of disemboweling the person you don't agree with to yourself. But I wasn't even in disagreement with anything. Just the opposite.

I was actually quite fascinated by Mark.

THE SNIPER

He was everything...I wasn't.

Or rather—

he was everything I didn't give myself permission to be. He had gone out and tested the waters of that side of ourselves that we're taught to keep under lock and key. And these people who do that, who test those waters, we call — heroes. Because that's what heroes are, right? In myths. Those who leave the norm — what's normal and safe and venture out to do battle, and supposedly return that much wiser and further ahead than those who just gab like me. And when he told me he had been selected to be a sniper because he had a knack for it...I just nodded.

And smiled.

And asked if he wanted a drink, because at that point I was getting way too involved and needed a breather. And when I returned with drinks, I asked *more* questions. Without wanting to seem too eager. And I was, very eager. And these weren't the judgmental, how-could-you-do-that kind of questions, no:

these were the pornographic, peeping-Tom kind of questions. Why?

Because in my mind I was thinking, in spite of my beliefs and everything else, that...

this was the measure of a man.

I was talking to someone whom we all put on a pedestal as a measure of what a real man should be. I was a puny peacenik indeed. I was derelict in the duty of being a man. I was a non-man. He was talking about blowing people's heads off and I was thinking, he has a bigger dick than me. His was bigger, badder and fired real bullets. Perhaps there was something homoerotic after all. Maybe Joan was right. Maybe we need to do away with all this sublimating of our erotic impulses into war and just fuck. Fuck it out.

And it wasn't just me. When the others came, that's when I started to get wind of what was going on. When the others reacted just like me. This viper-nest of liberal do-gooders were drooling over this guy. And when I saw my own impulses writ large, I started to feel queasy, and wondered, what the hell is going on?

What was going on?

Were we just being polite, and welcoming? And inclusive?

No.

I think we all felt there was something more legitimate about this guy than us.

More real. More earnest. Something earned. He was the real deal and we were gas bags in comparison. But, you say, don't we support our troops? We always say that, "Support our troops". We're not going to be painted into the corner of being called unpatriotic. No, we're going to rally behind our soldiers and throw garlands around their necks when they come home. We really are more Christian than the Christians who just talk about loving the sinner and not the sin. We genuinely love the sinner, apparently.

That's our stand: we support our troops.

And…

I no longer know why the hell that is.

Because by the end of that evening, I realized that was…bullshit….

There is a major…a major disconnect here, Babs.

What the hell do we mean, "We support our troops"?

What does that mean?…

THE SNIPER

What the fuck does that mean?

We're saying—us peace-activists, so-called, we're saying, that we love the sinner and condemn the sin? Then that really is being as hypocritical as the Evangelicals because you know in their hearts they can't stand the sinner. In fact, I think we're more truthful in truly loving the sinner and—what I'm saying is…we shouldn't.

We shouldn't love the sinner, in this case.

You can't separate the two. You can't separate war and the soldiers who fight in it. That's stupid. It's—. It's stupid. The reason why we don't have any teeth in this movement is because we're straddling this insane fence. You can't say no to war and say yes to the troops who make it possible.

Soldiers are, *they are the war machine*. What are we doing when we say we support the troops? This isn't theory. Aren't we—? Aren't we saying yes to everything we oppose by saying joining the war machine is just fine?

And what I began to think,

as I saw us pandering to this guy,

drooling over him, is that everyone there was on some elemental level saying that war is probably inevitable and so let's not get too worked up over the killers in our midst.

Because the guy was a killer.

He was trained to…to kill. Efficiently.

We were having drinks and dinner with a…

with a killer.

We made room at the dinner table and in our hearts for this—highly decorated, licensed killer. And I know you'll probably think, "Oh come on, what were you going to do, throw him out? Embarrass him?" No. And I know this sounds like I'm being—I don't know—elitist—or not being sympathetic to what may have forced Mark to become an expert in blowing people's heads off. That rather than going on welfare or a low-paying job he succeeded in becoming a very useful member of our society. He learnt a skill. A somewhat specialized skill. Learning how to dehumanize and think badly enough of someone so that all he saw was a target. Something that had to be neutralized....

Don't be an activist snob, you might say.

Don't let your upbringing and class privilege get in the way of asking the man if he wants another drink. Better still, grow up. That's the problem with us wimps in the movement, we're too squeamish and utopian and unplugged from what's real to be of practical use to anyone; so yes, grow up.

And the grown-up thing to do is to behave exactly as we were at that party. Make small talk and politely inquire about his experience. Like we were getting a travel review from someone who'd gone on an exotic vacation.

And it was only late in the party, as I picked up from Mark, that far from feeling anything, he seemed to have quite enjoyed his stint behind the cross hairs.

And that whatever private reservations we might have been having, we must have also understood, if only unconsciously—that regardless of our personal beliefs, we—we'd given him that job. We were as complicit as he was.

He was standing there, in our midst, as our representative in the good fight to savage another person. Even as we railed against the war, we were ra-ra-ing the troops, because apparently—apparently they have zero responsibility. And maybe we were

THE SNIPER

oh-so polite because deep down we understood that these fucking contradictions of ours made our hands as bloody as his.

And when I finally asked him the only serious question the entire evening,

"Don't you feel any remorse for what you did?" … everyone just looked at me as if I had let out a giant fart. —There was an embarrassed silence. —And then Joan changed the subject, and on we went.

So—yes.

I would like to bring this up in the next meeting.

I don't think we should…I don't think we should support anything to do with the war. Or that makes war possible. I don't.

We should call it as it is. Anyone who joins up becomes a killer. He kills. That's what we ask of him, or her. Kill. Hate, dehumanize, maim; wipe out, snuff out, fuck-up, destroy, wreck, humiliate, obliterate. I *do* want my hands to be clean. I *do* want to be able to say with a clear conscience, you fucking asshole get out of the fucking military and stop being such a plague that destroys everything that makes life worth living. You don't save shit. And you can't play victim when *you're* the eight hundred pound gorilla. You're a fucking killer and you need to get out.

And say it in a non-confrontational way if possible.

"Be the thing you want to change", etc.

In fact I came out of that evening realizing I was more of a pacifist than I thought I was. In comparison to my fellow liberals at the party.

I just think that would get rid of a huge…elephant-sized—inconsistency. That nobody wants to talk about. "We support the troops." What does that mean?

Maybe you're holed up because you're seeing too many of these stupid, just—dumb-ass—not-thinking-things-through—patterns clogging up our ability to have any impact. So let's...let's figure this out together. Don't...let's not get separated. Or demoralized.

Okay? —Babs?

I wish you were here.

We could have made a night of it....

Call me.

We'll figure this out together.

Lots of love, okay? ...I love you. I wish you had been at the party.... Maybe you would have seen things differently.

(He switches off the recorder.... Considers saying more into the recorder...instead, he eats a chip. Blackout)

END OF PLAY

A MARRIAGE PROPOSAL
(adapted from Chekhov's farce)

A MARRIAGE PROPOSAL was first performed at the Arab Theatrical Arts Guild in Dearborn in 2001. The cast and creative contributor were:

MAGDI .... Kam Kewson
NABIL .... Edward M Nahat
DEENAH .... Sarab Kamoo

Director .... Abdulrahmen "Ray" Alcodray

A MARRIAGE PROPOSAL was later performed at Golden Thread Productions' ReOrient Festival in San Francisco in 2001. The cast and creative contributor were:

MAGDI .... Ted Herzberg
NABIL .... Thomas Lynam
DEENAH .... Deborah Davis-Price

Director .... Ana Bayat

CHARACTERS

MAGDI, *from 50s to 60s*
NABIL, *30s*
DEENAH, *30s*

(In the blackout, a doorbell is heard. Lights up. Off-stage we hear the voices of NABIL *and* MAGDI. *[Note to actors/ director: translate as much of the characters' English into Arabic as you feel is appropriate.])*

MAGDI: *(Off-stage)* What a lovely surprise. "Ahlan, ahlan. Fadal." Come in. Why have you stayed away so long? We've missed you.

NABIL: *(Off-stage)* Hello, "hadretek".

MAGDI: *(Off-stage)* Give me a kiss. Don't you kiss in America anymore?

(Sound of kissing)

MAGDI: *(Off-stage)* Why do you not visit more often?

*(*MAGDI *and* NABIL *enter.* MAGDI *is dressed in a comfortable "gallebeya".* NABIL *is dressed in a suit and tie.)*

MAGDI: I was asking Deenah, why doesn't Nabil visit more often? Are we strangers that he should not say hello?

NABIL: Well, I've been very—

MAGDI: To say hello. Is that so hard? Aren't our families one family. Sit down, sit down.

NABIL: *(He sits.)* Well I've been very—

MAGDI: Deenah thinks you're afraid I'll make you speak Arabic. Of course not. You are American. "Khalas". I won't torture you because you don't know the language of your family's country. Your mother's language. "Abuk's" language. The language of your grandmother and grandfather on both sides stretching back generations. It's a shame, yes, but I won't embarrass the boy, I tell her, just to remind him that he should be ashamed of himself. It's not his fault. His parents should have insisted. What's the matter? You don't look well.

NABIL: Can I have a glass of water, please?

MAGDI: "A'seer lemoon?" Better for your health.

NABIL: "Shukraan."

(MAGDI *walks over to a table with a pitcher of lemonade and glasses.* NABIL *takes out a pill-box and selects a pill.*)

MAGDI: *(To himself)* He's come to ask for money for sure. His family thinks they're too good for us. More educated, a better class. But when it comes to money? They sing another song. The only reason he visits. Well he won't get a piaster. Not a cent.
(To NABIL, *as he goes to him.)*
Lemons straight from the farm. I import them now, you know. They're selling very well.

NABIL: Thank you.
(He swallows the pill and drinks.)

MAGDI: Why the pills? You are too young for pills.

NABIL: It's nothing. It's—work—stress. The usual.

MAGDI: This country's hard for sure. You work or you're nothing. No "Inshallah", "bookra", or "ma'lish". And even who your family is counts for zero here.

NABIL: It's not that. It's, uhm…well, it's uhm…

MAGDI: It's what, my boy? Relax.

NABIL: If you'll allow me, I'll—I'll get straight to the point.

MAGDI: Absolutely. We're in America now. Unless you get straight to the point, there's no reason to talk. What is it?

A MARRIAGE PROPOSAL

NABIL: The thing is—the reason why I've come, and I'm sorry for not visiting more often, it's just that—well—never mind why. I keep meaning to and—well—I'm here now. And the reason why I'm here, "hadretek", is—previously, last time, you were very kind when I came to you with a request and I can't thank you enough for that. And, once again, I find myself—sitting before you with a request. Though I don't want you to think I only come when I want something, I don't. I mean, I do now. But that's not the reason why I'm here. It is, but I'd come when I don't if work wasn't so busy. Though I know that's no excuse.

MAGDI: And this point you wanted to get to is what?

NABIL: Excuse me?

MAGDI: You hinted you wanted to get to a point. I agreed with you. What is it?

NABIL: Yes, I'm—I'm getting to that.

MAGDI: Unless you no longer want to get to it. In which case we can have another glass of lemonade and watch T V.

NABIL: *(Mustering up the courage)* "Hadretek."

MAGDI: "Na'm."

NABIL: The thing is—

MAGDI: How much?

NABIL: How much what?

MAGDI: How much do you want? Is business not going well?

NABIL: Business is fine.

MAGDI: Then spit it out!

NABIL: I've come—I've come to ask for your daughter's hand in marriage.
(Slight beat)

I want to marry Deenah. With your permission.

(Beat. MAGDI *jumps up from his seat, which startles* NABIL. MAGDI's *eyes open wide, which also concerns* NABIL. MAGDI *walks over to him, which really worries* NABIL.*)*

NABIL: I mean if that's—if it's not—because if it is—then I can leave. —Oh God.

*(*MAGDI *yanks* NABIL *up from the couch.)*

MAGDI: Say it again.

NABIL: I don't have to if you don't want me to.

MAGDI: Say it again!

NABIL: I would like to marry Deenah. If you don't mind.

*(*MAGDI *grabs both* NABIL's *cheeks.)*

MAGDI: "Ibni."

(Kisses NABIL's *cheeks)*

My son! Do you know how long I have been hoping for this? Today, you are a man to me. Your father's son. A prince! At last, our two families will be together for sure.

NABIL: It's okay with you?

MAGDI: Okay? It's "ahsan min" okay. It's a dream come true.

NABIL: Do you think Deenah will agree?

MAGDI: Are you joking? She talks about nothing but you. She adores you. I'm going to go get her right now. She's crazy for you. You make me very proud. Don't move. Don't move.

*(*MAGDI *exits. Slight beat.* NABIL *holds up his shaking hands.)*

NABIL: *(To himself)* My God. I'm shaking. It's like taking a test. I have to slow down.

A MARRIAGE PROPOSAL

(Takes another pill with lemonade)
My heart's racing. Deep breath.
(Takes a deep breath)
Stay calm. The main thing is to make up my mind and stick to it. If I think about it too much it won't happen. She's a good match. She's pretty, charming. And Egyptian. My parents want me to marry an Egyptian. I'll marry an Egyptian. She may be a little "balady", a little country, but that's good. It'll keep me in touch with my roots. On top of that she speaks perfect English. Oh God I'm so nervous. My ears are buzzing. I have to slow down.
(Drinks lemonade and makes a semi-gagging gesture)
These lemons are disgusting. I can't believe anyone buys this crap. Label something "From The Middle East" and people think they're getting something unique. Nabil…think calm, be calm. You're thirty-five and you have to settle down. This is why you're so nervous all the time. There's no stability in your life. Marrying her will give you that stability. It might even improve your health. After all—you know her. You're comfortable with her. You both have compatible dispositions—

(DEENAH enters. She has an apron on over her clothes.)

DEENAH: Oh. It's only you. Baba just said a friend had come to see me.

NABIL: So I have.

DEENAH: It's been a while since we've seen you. "Izeyak?" Please sit down. Have you eaten? I hope you'll stay for lunch.

NABIL: Thank you, I can't.

DEENAH: Would you like some lemonade?

NABIL: I've had some, thanks.

(They both sit down.)

DEENAH: Excuse my apron, I've been making "kofta".
I bet it's been a while since you've eaten real "kofta".
The way I make it.

NABIL: It has, yes.

DEENAH: And for dessert I'm making "Om Ali".

NABIL: You are?

DEENAH: It's your favorite isn't it?

NABIL: Yes it is.

DEENAH: Then don't be silly and stay for lunch.

NABIL: Alright. Thank you. I will.

DEENAH: What's the matter, Nabil? You look pale. Is everything alright at work?

NABIL: Yes. Yes it is. Deenah...the reason why I've come—

DEENAH: Must you have a reason to visit? This is your home. I worry about you, with your family so far away. Living alone.

NABIL: Thank you, I'm—. Well: the reason why I've stayed away so long is that it's taken me a while to come to, finally, to come to a decision. Not that I've had to think about it, it was an easy decision to make; except it *is* a big step, and for all I know it might not be to your liking.

DEENAH: What are you talking about?

NABIL: Let me get to the point. Our families... Deenah—since childhood, our childhood, have known each other, and have always had the greatest respect for each other. And our paths always—well, they always seem to cross. I move here, then your family moves here and sets up a business. And before that, when your father bought the land next to ours. So that our apples would fall into your lemon grove; and your lemons would roll into our orchard. Almost as if they wanted to mix and be together as well. Like there was a romance going on even between our trees.

DEENAH: *(Smiling at the memory)* Yes. Except that problem was solved when we bought the apple orchard.

NABIL: I'm sorry?

DEENAH: Don't you remember? You wouldn't, of course, we were kids, but it happened very soon after we bought the land next to yours. It was decided it'd be easier for everyone if we bought your apple orchard.

NABIL: Are we—talking about the apple orchard next to the road?

DEENAH: Yes.

NABIL: Between the road and the stream?

DEENAH: That's right. The way your orchard stuck out into our property, it was decided it would be simpler to make them part of the sale.

NABIL: *(Slight beat)* Really? I think you—may want to check on that. Because last I heard, they're…I mean—I understand why you may *think* that.

DEENAH: Think what?

NABIL: That it's yours.

DEENAH: It is ours.

NABIL: *(Slight beat)* You mean the orchard where I used to bring my play things in the summer? And put up my tent?

DEENAH: We didn't mind you doing that. Even though you never let me play with you. Which I thought was mean of you at the time.

NABIL: I'm sorry I didn't let you play with me, but—that orchard—if we're talking about the same orchard—

DEENAH: There is only one apple orchard.

NABIL: Well—then—it's ours. I mean I'm trying to think how there might be a misunderstanding.

DEENAH: Nabil. That orchard has been with my family for thirty years.

NABIL: Not really. No.

DEENAH: *(Still on the light side)* Nabil, stop it.

NABIL: I can show you the deed. Now that I think about it, my father did mention to me once that there had been a minor dispute about it. But the matter was resolved.

DEENAH: Yes, in our favor. That orchard belongs to us. I don't understand why you'd say it doesn't. You didn't come here to argue about that, did you?

NABIL: No. It's not important. I'm just saying, for the record. Otherwise it makes no difference.

DEENAH: You're right. It isn't important. But for the record, if we're talking about the record then: it's ours.

NABIL: *(Slight beat)* Deenah...uhm...actually...it belongs—it belongs to my family.

DEENAH: You're teasing me.

NABIL: Not yet.

DEENAH: Why would I make this up?

NABIL: I don't think you would. I just think you're misinformed.

DEENAH: You're the "khawaga", Nabil, who left twenty years ago. I've been picking apples from that orchard before and after you left.

A MARRIAGE PROPOSAL

NABIL: That's because we let you pick them. It wasn't a business concern of ours, so it didn't matter.

DEENAH: You *are* making fun of me.

NABIL: I'm not. But I think that's where the misunderstanding comes from. Because year after year we allowed you to pick from our trees. —But anyway, it's not important.

DEENAH: It's not. But for the record, for the sake of facts, because it's clear you're not aware of them, that orchard is ours. I don't know why you've suddenly got it into your head they're not. Maybe you miss home and are feeling very attached to everything you remember.

NABIL: I can show you the deed.

DEENAH: Nabil, enough. Your teasing is not nice anymore.

NABIL: I don't care about it, honestly, I don't. It's just— as a matter of principle.

DEENAH: I agree. Those acres aren't worth anything, but as a matter of principle, yes, it matters.

NABIL: Fine. Look, we'll—I'll give them to you. If it's that important. Maybe you and your father would like to import the apples as well and sell them here. You know. Perhaps the lemons aren't doing too well.

DEENAH: The lemons are selling very nicely, thank you.

NABIL: As what, mouthwash?

(If DEENAH *hasn't stood up before, she stands up now.)*

DEENAH: I don't know why you're behaving this way. You've acted strangely from the moment you said hello. What's got into you? We've always considered you a good neighbor, even family, in Egypt, and here. Even if you do think you're too good for us sometimes.

Though obviously not when it comes to borrowing money from us.

(If NABIL *hasn't stood up before, he stands up now.)*

NABIL: I intend to give back every cent of that loan.

DEENAH: When? As a business man you're terrible. You're a better dreamer. And your family isn't much better, to be frank. We had to postpone expanding our stores because of that loan. You're being very rude if you're being serious. Giving us our land back. We'll give them to you!

NABIL: They're not yours to give.

DEENAH: Yes they *are*.

NABIL: No they're not.

DEENAH: Stop it.

NABIL: You stop it.

DEENAH: I'll give them to you this very day.

NABIL: You can keep your offer. They're already ours.

DEENAH: Then all I can say is you're a liar. You were always a spoilt brat and now we can add liar to your accomplishments.

NABIL: You're calling me a liar?

DEENAH: What's the matter, don't you understand English either?

NABIL: Alright, fine. I'll prove it to you.
(Moves to the phone.)
I'll call the farm right now and tell them to start picking the apples. I'll tell them to send them to your stores.

DEENAH: I'll have them thrown off the land and call collect!

NABIL: *(Slams down phone)* I'll use my cell-phone!

A MARRIAGE PROPOSAL

DEENAH: You can use your "teezak" and send smoke signals for all I care!

NABIL: *(Dialing cell-phone)* I'll show you who owns what.

DEENAH: And don't you raise your voice in my house. Or are you going to tell me this house is yours as well!

NABIL: I wouldn't want it, you have lousy taste. And I'm not shouting. If my heart wasn't palpitating the way it is, I wouldn't be reacting as calmly as I'm doing now. For the last time, that orchard is ours.

DEENAH: Ours!

NABIL: It's ours!

(MAGDI *enters.*)

MAGDI: "E-da, e-da?" What's the matter? Why all this shouting?

DEENAH: Baba. Please tell this idiot who owns the apple orchard.

MAGDI: Deenah. That's no way to speak to anybody. Especially not Nabil.

DEENAH: Then tell this *gentleman* who owns the orchard.

MAGDI: The apple orchard? The orchard is ours.

NABIL: But "hadretek", how can you say that? Be fair. I understand how year after year when you and your workers picked the apples you might come to believe you owned the land, but in fact—

MAGDI: Oh no, my son, what you forget, and you were too young at the time, is that there *was* a question at the beginning about what we should do: draw a half circle around the orchard, or a straight line down the middle and include the trees. Which is what we did. It was the simplest solution. The matter has been settled for years. Everyone knows that orchard belong to the Ganzari's.

NABIL: But...I can prove to you it's ours.

MAGDI: That would be very interesting to see.

NABIL: We have the deed.

MAGDI: I think maybe it's because you've been away so long.

NABIL: Would everyone stop saying that! I'm not a "khawaga"!

MAGDI: *(Trying to calm him)* Yes, alright, alright.

NABIL: And even if I am, you can't convince me that what is a *fact isn't* just because I can't speak Arabic.

MAGDI: My son, keep calm.

NABIL: I *am* calm.

MAGDI: You were always a little "nervis".

NABIL: I had no idea you were under this delusion.

MAGDI: I'm not after anything of yours, and I don't intend to give up anything of mine. Why should I? But if we're going to argue about it, it's not worth it. Not for a second. It would be better to give the land back to the "fellaheen" who work on it now.

NABIL: But—you can't give away something that isn't yours. With all due respect, you don't have that right.

MAGDI: I think I ought to know if I have the right or not. And I should also tell you I'm not used to being spoken to in that tone of voice. I am twice your age and I ask you to please speak to me in a calm manner.

NABIL: I'm being told that what has belonged to my family for hundreds of years is suddenly yours? And you expect me to stay calm? You must think I'm a fool. Why, because I borrowed money from you? Well at least I *borrowed* it, I didn't *steal* it.

A MARRIAGE PROPOSAL

(A slight gasp from DEENAH *and* MAGDI.*)*

MAGDI: What do you mean by that? *What do you mean by that?*

DEENAH: Call up the farm, baba. Tell them to pick those apples this very instant.

NABIL: *(Holding up cell-phone)* Try it and they'll be met by the police!

MAGDI: What did you say?!

DEENAH: He called us thieves! In our own house!

NABIL: I said unlike *some* people the Bemyehs have never stolen anything in their lives. And I'll go to the courts if I have to prove that orchard is ours!

MAGDI: You can go to court and "sitteen dehya" for all I care! It's what your family does best. Suing and taking money away from honest, hardworking families. If you didn't force people to settle out of court, you wouldn't have a penny to your name.

NABIL: My family are *honorable* people and not one of them was *ever* tried for embezzlement, unlike some people I know.

MAGDI: Don't you dare speak my father's name. Don't you dare!

DEENAH: You're a fine one to talk with your good-for-nothing family who do nothing but live off their good name which everyone knows was bought for with bribes.

NABIL: That's a lie! Take that back!

MAGDI: It's the truth!

*(*NABIL *starts to clutch his chest as if experiencing chest pains.)*

DEENAH: And what have *you* accomplished after twenty years in America? You've a failed business, no family, and you even had to go on welfare.

NABIL: That wasn't welfare, you idiot, that was a *grant*. It's a prize.

(NABIL *takes out his pill-box.*)

MAGDI: *(Derisive)* Ha!

DEENAH: We've been here four years and have two successful stores.

NABIL: That's because you bought those stores in depressed neighborhoods where people are desperate. It's people like you who give us a bad name.
(*He swallows a couple of pills.*)

MAGDI: Don't you speak to me about bad names, you and your drunkard sisters; and your aunt, your married aunt who ran off with a farm-hand.

NABIL: She's a socialist! It was matter of principle and ideology. And who are you to throw stones with an uncle who was arrested for indecent exposure!

DEENAH: He couldn't find a restroom! He had a bladder infection!

NABIL: Only four years in America and a Ganzari in jail.

MAGDI: Indecency? With your grandfather who wouldn't let a day go by without grabbing the asses of his workers.

NABIL: At least I know for sure who *my* grandfather was.

(*Gasps from* DEENAH *and* MAGDI.)

DEENAH: Get out!

MAGDI: "Ya ibn kalb!"

DEENAH: Get out you mean, spiteful—

A MARRIAGE PROPOSAL

MAGDI: "Ya sharmoot!"
(And other Arabic expletives)

NABIL: You can't kick me out, I'm going! Where's the door? Oh God, my heart.

DEENAH: *(Overlapping)* Get out!

NABIL: My foot's gone numb. I have to get out.

DEENAH: Go on, get out!

MAGDI: All your family's worthless! They don't add up to shit. Not even shit. Shit I can use for fertilizer.

NABIL: Goodbye. You'll be hearing from my lawyers. *(He exits.)*

DEENAH: Not before you hear from ours!

MAGDI: *(Following him out, off-stage.)* And don't you ever, *ever* enter my house again!

NABIL: *(Off-stage)* Not if you paid me.

MAGDI: *(Off-stage)* Knowing how bankrupt you are, yes you would!

(The door is slammed. MAGDI *comes back in. Note: In this next section between* DEENAH *and* MAGDI, *actors/director may want to add more Arabic words/phrases than indicated in the text. Or not, depending on the audience.)*

DEENAH: What a horrible, horrible man he is.

MAGDI: Like his family. They can all go to hell!

DEENAH: I hate him!

MAGDI: This country's made him mad—madder than he was before.

DEENAH: First he tries to steal our land and then he screams at you, and insults you. I could kick him. I could really just punch him.

MAGDI: And to think he came here to propose to you. Propose! *Him*. My son-in-law. Imagine! What a nightmare that would have been.

(MAGDI *goes over to drink a glass of lemonade.* DEENAH *stops and stares at her father. Slight beat*)

DEENAH: Propose?

MAGDI: It would have been a catastrophe—that never ends!

DEENAH: Propose what?

MAGDI: Marriage! He wanted to marry you. He came here to ask for your hand. We must give special thanks to God, *special* thanks that He opened his mouth and showed us who this man really is.

DEENAH: He came here to propose to me?

MAGDI: Yes, I'm telling you.

DEENAH: He wants to…he wants to marry me?

MAGDI: Don't worry. It's alright. You're saved. He'll never enter this house again.

(DEENAH *looks like she might be in pain. She clutches her stomach.*)

MAGDI: Deenah. What's the matter? It's finished. You'll never see him again, I promise you.

(*This triggers a more anguished look on* DEENAH's *face.*)

MAGDI: Speak to me. Forgive me. I should never have let him in.

DEENAH: *(Strangled voice)* Bring…bring him back.

MAGDI: Bring who back?

(DEENAH *frantically points to the door before she can speak.*)

DEENAH: *(Strangled voice)* Bring him back. Back. Get him. Bring him—get—. Get him back!

MAGDI: Who?

A MARRIAGE PROPOSAL

DEENAH: Is there anyone else who's come here today to propose to me you haven't told me about?

MAGDI: Nabil? What do you want Nabil for?

DEENAH: To marry me!

MAGDI: You want him to—? You want to marry him?!

DEENAH: *(Anguished cry)* Yes!

MAGDI: What have I done to deserve this day.

DEENAH: I feel sick. I want to die.

MAGDI: I'm going to hang myself. I want to shoot myself. But first, I'm going to hang myself.

DEENAH: Get him. Bring him back!

MAGDI: How can I? We've ruined your chances.

DEENAH: Baba!

MAGDI: Don't yell at me! You're all crazy! Completely "magnoon!" What a horrible life!

(MAGDI *exits.* DEENAH *tries to calm down. She goes over to the pitcher of lemonade. She starts to pour herself a glass, but then doesn't bother and drinks straight from the pitcher. She removes her apron and throws it off stage. She straightens her hair. She throws off her worn slippers and runs off-stage as he returns.)*

MAGDI: He's coming back, the little snake. I don't want to look at him. You talk to him.

(DEENAH *returns hopping as she puts on new shoes.)*

DEENAH: Bring him back!

MAGDI: He's coming back I said! If only your mother was alive, she would know what to do. You'll be the death of me!

DEENAH: What did he say?

MAGDI: What do you think? We insulted him, we cursed him, and kicked him out. He's not happy. And all because of your temper.

DEENAH: Me? It was all your fault.

MAGDI: My fault?

DEENAH: If only you'd told me he wanted to marry me right at the beginning.

(NABIL *enters, panting slightly.*)

MAGDI: Here's his highness. Talk to him yourself. I've had enough. Why me?
(He exits.)

DEENAH: Nabil.

NABIL: Deenah. I—I'm—

DEENAH: Nabil.

NABIL: I can't take this. I'm not used to this—this abuse. I'm not well. My doctor has expressly told me to take it easy. I have a cramp in my side right now.

DEENAH: Why don't you sit down. Sit. Let me get you a—
(Turns to the lemonade.)
Never mind.

NABIL: And my heart. And for some reason my foot has gone completely asleep.

DEENAH: You must forgive us. We all just got too excited. I remember now. The apple orchard *is* yours, of course it is.

NABIL: And my eyebrows, look, they're twitching. They've never twitched like that before.

DEENAH: We were wrong. The orchard is definitely yours.

NABIL: It is.

A MARRIAGE PROPOSAL

DEENAH: It is yours. Baba and I realized this the moment you left. We were mistaken, that's all. It happens.

NABIL: I only argued on principle. The land isn't worth much at all, but the principle.

(DEENAH *and* NABIL *sit on the couch.*)

DEENAH: Agreed. I agree.

NABIL: Otherwise I would never have gone on.

DEENAH: Why don't we change the subject. We'll talk of something nicer.

NABIL: And I have evidence. I can show it to you.

DEENAH: There's no need.

NABIL: So you know for sure.

(DEENAH *squeezes* NABIL's *arm or leg a little too tightly.*)

DEENAH: I *know*. Let's drop it, okay?

NABIL: Okay—ow.

DEENAH: It's been so long since you've seen your parents. Aren't you going back to visit soon? Don't you miss hunting in the winter? Do you remember we were the only people in the entire area who liked to hunt. "There's nothing to hunt", they'd say. But we always found something. That's an activity both our families enjoyed. We should plan a trip together and do it again. Would you like that?

NABIL: That would be nice, yes. It's been years since I've done that. You know my hunting dog "Torshy" died.

DEENAH: I'm sorry to hear that. He was getting old wasn't he?

NABIL: They told me he ate something poisonous and died.

DEENAH: I'm so sorry.
(Rubs or pats his arm.)
I know how much you loved him. It's hard to replace animals that have become part of the family. I felt the same way about ours. But you'll find another dog. I'll help you pick one out if you want.

NABIL: It won't be so easy to find another one with his qualities. You know we paid a thousand pounds for him.

(DEENAH is startled by the amount.)

NABIL: He came to us from a kennel in England.

DEENAH: A thousand pounds? That's too much, isn't it?

NABIL: Not for his pedigree. It was a bargain, actually. He was a first class dog.

DEENAH: Baba only paid a hundred pounds for "Bungar" and—for my money anyway, he was as good a hunter as "Torshy". In my opinion. Plus he was Egyptian.

NABIL: Egyptian or not, with all respect to "Bungar", he was a house-dog you took out on the hunt with you. He had good points, but, hunting was not one of them. "Torshy" was bred to hunt.

DEENAH: That may be. But, if you remember, "Torshy" usually appeared only *after* "Bungar" had done the work of cornering the rabbit. If it wasn't for "Bungar", "Torshy" couldn't have found his own tail, let alone another animal. To be honest. —If we're being honest.

NABIL: *(Slight beat)* I guess that's your interpretation. But what is a fact, is, your dog, as sweet as he was, and I know you were attached to him, had no pedigree. He was a mongrel, basically. And was overshot. And overshot dogs are bad hunters.

A MARRIAGE PROPOSAL

DEENAH: Overshot? This is the first I've heard of it. What does "overshot" mean?

NABIL: It means the lower jaw is shorter than the upper.

DEENAH: Oh? Really? You measured them?

NABIL: It's alright for pointing, but if you want him to retrieve…

DEENAH: First of all, "Bungar" was not a mongrel. And secondly, the English cheated you. They probably gave you a story about their dog being bred for fox-hunting on some English manor and you believed them. And thirdly, why did you look abroad for a dog when in Egypt you have a very good selection?

NABIL: "Bungar" was a terrier, basically. Terriers aren't Egyptian.

DEENAH: He was born in Egypt. Several generations back.

NABIL: I don't care how far back he goes, he was a terrible hunter and had bad breath.

(DEENAH *stands, agitated.*)

DEENAH: What is the matter with you today? You want to find a quarrel in everything. First you tell us the apple orchard is yours and now you want to say your dog was superior to ours when everyone knows "Bungar" was a better hunter *and* better groomed than your flea-bitten beagle.

NABIL: How would you know? You always turned your head away before the hunt ended.

DEENAH: Because I hated seeing the rabbit get killed.

NABIL: So you don't know.

DEENAH: I didn't have to see the end of it to know.

NABIL: But you *don't* know. And the fact remains he was overshot.

DEENAH: You have no clue what you're talking about.

NABIL: You don't even know what that means.

DEENAH: It's enough to know what you mean.

NABIL: You can't argue a fact.

DEENAH: You can when it's a lie!

NABIL: *(Gets up)* Alright, I've had it. I'm going. *(He clutches his chest.)*

DEENAH: You talk such nonsense half the time I don't even know why I listen to you.

NABIL: I have to go. My pulse; my heart. It's going to burst.

DEENAH: *(Overlapping)* And it's funny how the hunters who do the most arguing don't know a thing about it.

NABIL: *Shut up.* Can't you see I'm ill!

DEENAH: I'm not going to shut up until you stop making these stupid claims!

NABIL: Why are you shouting?! My heart's falling apart! Shut up!

DEENAH: You shut up!

(MAGDI *enters.*)

MAGDI: What is the matter now?

DEENAH: Baba.
(Takes a breath)
Baba…will you please tell us in your objective opinion,
(To NABIL*)*
and we both know my father can be objective,
(To MAGDI*)*
who the better hunter was: "Bungar" or "Torshy".

A MARRIAGE PROPOSAL

MAGDI: *(Slight beat)* You're arguing about dogs? — "Kalaab"?

DEENAH: It's important.

NABIL: "Hadretek." Please: tell me just one thing before you answer. Wasn't your dog, as loyal and special as he was, wasn't he overshot?

MAGDI: What does overshot mean?

DEENAH: It means the lower jaw is shorter than the upper.

MAGDI: What does that have to do with anything?

DEENAH: Precisely.

NABIL: It means he was not a good retriever, which is what a hunting dog is supposed to do: retrieve.

MAGDI: Retrieve, not retrieve, who cares. They're both dead. We're not hunting anymore.

DEENAH: But baba, he insulted him. You loved "Bungar".

NABIL: I didn't insult him. I was pointing out canine physiology.

DEENAH: You said he was inferior to your dog.

NABIL: Any dog expert will tell you what I said. I'm not saying he was a *bad* dog.

MAGDI: Dog expert? What kind of job is dog expert? Who cares? What I know for sure, if you're serious about it is that yes, your dog was a good hunter, and so was ours. "Bungar", because he was a real "fellah". And maybe because he was not as refined as yours, he was not afraid to jump in when things got dangerous. Whereas your "Torshy" would hold back.

NABIL: But how can you say that? "Torshy" never held back. He was faster than your dog.

MAGDI: I'm not talking about speed, but character. And courage. And if he wasn't as fast, that has to do with the fact that on one hunt, your father whipped him very hard. He never recovered from that, but never mind, we forgave you for it.

NABIL: That's because he was chasing sheep, when we were hunting something else. If my father hadn't whipped him, he would've chased the sheep into the next field.

(MAGDI *grabs* NABIL *by the lapels.* MAGDI *tries not to shout.*)

MAGDI: What is the matter with you? Has this country pickled your brain? Do you have an American stick up your ass that you should talk to me like this?

DEENAH: *(Trying to restrain her father)* Baba.

MAGDI: Are we not good enough for you? Not American enough? "ya ibn kalb". Enough!

(MAGDI *lets* NABIL *go.*)

MAGDI: No more talking about dogs. I will not lose my temper over this. Are we so jealous about what someone else has that we should argue about dogs? Does it make us so blind? Yes, obviously it does. Or you'd see your dog was a piece of shit who spent the time hunting smelling my dog's asshole!

DEENAH: *(To* NABIL*)* You see. He remembers.

MAGDI: I remember the whole business!

(NABIL *is indignant to the point of being short of breath.*)

NABIL: I remember it too. How dare you.

MAGDI: *(Mocking)* "I remember it too." What do you remember? You have no memory about your country. You look down on your country.

(NABIL *starts experiencing chest pains again.*)

A MARRIAGE PROPOSAL

MAGDI: Look at you. Holding your heart like it's going to fall out. You should be at home hunting cockroaches!

DEENAH: I don't know why he wants to argue everything. Coming here and picking a fight with us.

MAGDI: No more! Enough fighting! This is my house and I order everyone to change the subject!
(To NABIL*)*
You have no business talking about hunting. You were never a hunter and that's that.

NABIL: And you were? You couldn't walk a hundred yards without wanting a picnic break. The only reason you hunted was because you thought it impressed the neighbors. You thought we wouldn't take you for the uneducated "hamar" you are. Well it didn't work!

(Gasps from MAGDI *and* DEENAH*)*

MAGDI: I'll show you hunting, I'll shoot you down right now. With my bare fists if I have to!

DEENAH: How dare you speak to my father like that.

MAGDI: Did you hear what he called me? I can't believe my ears!

DEENAH: *(Overlapping) You're* the mongrel "kalb", you hateful man, with your half American, half Egyptian, and not a decent word of Arabic. You're pathetic!

NABIL: "Tuz" Arabic!

MAGDI: "Tuz" Arabic?
(To DEENAH*)*
The gun! Get the gun!
(He starts to exit.)

NABIL: *(Breathing hard)* And each of my halves is better than the whole of your family. Long live mongrels, I say!

(MAGDI *wheels around. He grabs the oranges, bananas and lemons from the bowl of fruit and throws them at* NABIL.)

MAGDI: "Ya hit'tit khara", I'll shoot you down this instant. You and your entire pack of mongrel Bemyehs!

(NABIL *tries to duck the flying fruit. He heads for the door but suddenly freezes. He clutches his heart and falls to his knees.*)

DEENAH: *(Alarmed)* Baba!

(MAGDI *stops throwing.*)

DEENAH: Baba!

MAGDI: "Tuz" him! "Tuz" his entire family!

(NABIL *collapses onto the floor.*)

DEENAH: He's dead!

MAGDI: Finally! He has done something right for once! "Alhamdulillah!"

DEENAH: *(Goes to* NABIL*)* He's really dead!

MAGDI: Don't bet on it. The Bemyehs never keep their promise. If he's dead, he'll wake up and break his word.

DEENAH: We killed him. Get a doctor!

MAGDI: What's he doing out of doors? He shouldn't move from his bed, the weakling. And he talks to me about hunting.

DEENAH: Get a doctor! Get a doctor!

(MAGDI *goes over and grabs the pitcher of lemonade.* DEENAH *is trying to revive* NABIL *by gently slapping his face.*)

MAGDI: What a life! What a miserable life! I should have shot myself a long time ago. I don't know what I'm waiting for.

(*He pours some lemonade on* NABIL's *face.*)

DEENAH: Baba. Baba. Look. He's waking up. He's coming to.

MAGDI: There! What did I tell you. How can you trust them? They never die. They just come back to torment us.

DEENAH: Give me the lemonade.

(MAGDI *pours the remaining lemonade onto* NABIL's *face. Or, another alternative: instead of the pitcher, he brings over a sliced lemon and squeezes that over* NABIL's *face.*)

DEENAH: Baba, stop!

NABIL: *(Disoriented)* Where am I?

DEENAH: *(Cradling his head)* Oh, thank God. Thank God you're alive.

MAGDI: Quick. Quick! Marry him this instant before he says something stupid again and I have to kill him.

(*As he says this,* MAGDI *kneels and places* NABIL's *hand in* DEENAH's *hand.*)

MAGDI: She accepts. I give you my blessing. On the condition you leave me in peace!

NABIL: Who accepts? What happened?

MAGDI: I said my daughter accepts. Kiss her and be done with it.

DEENAH: I accept...I accept, Nabil.

NABIL: You do?

MAGDI: Do you want to argue about it?

NABIL: *(Smiling, slight beat)* Not yet.

(*Perhaps they kiss.*)

MAGDI: At last. May you have argued all the quarrels you may ever have and now live in peace. "Inshallah."

NABIL: Deenah.

DEENAH: Nabil.

NABIL: I am very happy.

DEENAH: I'm happy too.

MAGDI: "Khalasna!"

(MAGDI *plops down on the couch. He peels and eats the banana he was holding.*)

DEENAH: I don't want to ever argue with you again.

NABIL: Why argue? I don't want to argue.

DEENAH: We can buy a dog—if you want. We'll love him together. You can pick him out. I want you to pick him out.

NABIL: The apple orchard will always be yours.

DEENAH: I don't want anything, it's enough that we marry.

NABIL: Well it's yours anyway.

DEENAH: Keep it. It's my wedding present to you.

NABIL: Deenah: why rob me of my desire to give you something?

DEENAH: "Rob" you?

NABIL: I want to show you how much you mean to me. I want to be generous to you, always.

DEENAH: But...since it's *our* orchard even though we're pretending it's yours that wouldn't be much of a demonstration of generosity, would it.

NABIL: Deenah.

DEENAH: Why are you doing this?

MAGDI: *(Rising from couch)* You two are fruits of the same kind and belong in the same orchard. The madhouse orchard. More lemonade! It's time to celebrate! *(He exits into the kitchen.)*

NABIL: You are *so* obstinate.

DEENAH: You're the one who's obstinate.

NABIL: I don't want to hear anymore about it. Like it or not it's yours.

DEENAH: Yours!

NABIL: It's yours!

(Blackout)

END OF PLAY

THE REVIEW

THE REVIEW was presented by Golden Thread Productions simultaneously via Skype in both Cairo and San Francisco in 2009. The cast and creative contributors were:

SHADIYAH ....Zaynab Magdy
RATIB ....James Asher
Directors ....Dina Amin (Cairo)
                                        Hafiz Karmali (San Francisco)

CHARACTERS

SHADIYAH, *20s or 30s*
RATIB, *20s or 30s*

NOTE

While this play was originally performed using Skype, casting the character of Shadiyah in Cairo, and projecting her image onto a large screen in the San Francisco theater, it is obviously more practical to cast the actor locally. Either you could 1) project the image of Shadiyah onto a screen (with the actor off-stage), or 2) have Shadiyah on stage and project both their images onto a screen, or 3) just have both characters at their computers with no images projected. Also, while there are references to Cairo, the character of Shadiyah can be from any Middle-Eastern country going through changes. In which case, simply change the Cairo references to the appropriate country.

(RATIB *is seated at a desk in front of his computer Skyping with* SHADIYAH. *He wears a bathrobe. There is a stuffed bear on the table, or somewhere nearby.*)

(SHADIYAH *is seen reading a manuscript.* RATIB *waits.*)

(Long beat)

RATIB: When you take a long pause like that I know what you're about to say is probably going to be flat-out horrible.

SHADIYAH: *(Not looking up from the story)* Can you shut up? Please?

RATIB: But that's fine. Just so you know I want you to be absolutely honest. Since the last story I sent you, I am, with the help of that therapist I mentioned, and daily meditation, I am much, *much* better able to take in criticism. I mean, really hear it. So please: be absolutely frank. Ignore the way I've reacted in the past. Part of the reason for sending you this story is not just to get your feedback, but a test—to prove to you, *and* myself, that I'm able to hear, really hear your evaluation without throwing a hissy-fit, or bitching. Or accusing you of whatever in other aspects of our relationship, like—that—ridiculous accusation that you were seeing someone else, and again my hundredth apology for that. I'm actually quite excited to take this new me out for a test drive, *especially* if you don't like the story. Hell for me is no longer when someone hates something I've written. That's actually the chrysalis phase, so to speak, in which the caterpillar, the story you're holding, can be improved and turned into a glorious butterfly. That flits from one grateful reader to another. So frankness, please. Otherwise, how can I truly believe you if you genuinely love the story.

SHADIYAH: Why are your stories always about the same thing? —It feels like you have the same characters in roughly the same situations, with just different names and locations. The past four or five stories.

RATIB: *(Slight beat)* Huh. Okay.

SHADIYAH: It's not even variations on a theme. It's really almost the exact same story. I've seen these characters before. Exact same set up.

RATIB: Okay. —You think so?

SHADIYAH: You have the ball-breaking bitch. Usually she's an Arab woman, sometimes not. And you're always undermining the sexuality of the Arab guy.

RATIB: Really?

SHADIYAH: If I was an Arab guy, I have to tell you, I'd be really insulted. As an Arab woman *I'm* insulted. I don't like seeing my men-folk being slammed like that. For instance:
(Reading)
"She looked at his shriveling member in its post-coital state and wondered what she ever saw in him in the first place." What is up with you giving your Arab men problematic genitalia? It feels like a constant in your stories.

RATIB: I'm—describing what happens after sex. To any guy's equipment. How that becomes a metaphor from her point of view.

SHADIYAH: Seriously, there's always something wrong.

RATIB: There's nothing *wrong* with it, she just latches onto the post-coital sagging as a sign of where she thinks their relationship is going.

THE REVIEW

SHADIYAH: *(Leafing through the story)* The self-loathing, it's too much. And the woman's always having an affair behind the guys's back. She's a ball-breaker, a cheater, and always cutting the guy down.

RATIB: You've applauded my championing of Arab women.

SHADIYAH: *No.* I'm sick of these depictions of quote unquote "strong women" who belittle the men in their lives.

RATIB: I happen to like strong, independent women.

SHADIYAH: No you don't, you *fear* them. That's why they always comes across as way too aggressive. And it's always at the expense of the Arab guy. So the reader comes away with a distorted view of the whole culture.

RATIB: Okay. Wait a minute. Are these—reservations? You have with the story? With its point of view? But which on the whole you like? Aesthetically speaking?

SHADIYAH: *(Still leafing through pages as she speaks)* No. I have to tell you, it's kind of rubbish. Which makes me reevaluate other things you've sent me. I think you need to start asking hard questions about the direction your writing is heading. I don't know if I just misread your past work; or it was because we'd just started going out and I was still infatuated. But your stories seem like they're starting to miss a big, central— *something*. Either they're not what they used to be, or they never were. To be frank.

RATIB: *(Slight beat)* Good. That's the frankness I'm looking for. Can you hold on a second?

(His chair having wheels, RATIB *pushes away from the computer screen so he's no longer seen by* SHADIYAH. *He puts his head in his hands. Then, perhaps, he moves to the stuffed bear seated on the table, or nearby, and slams the*

bear's head against the table. Then, to further expunge the emotions he's feeling, a second time. —Or maybe it's enough just to put his head in his hands.)

SHADIYAH: *(Still looking at the story)* You know what it is...with the last four or five stories of yours...

(RATIB *moves back to the computer screen and waits for her to speak. Finally:)*

RATIB: *(Trying to control his irritation)* What?

SHADIYAH: I'm trying to find a way to put this delicately.

RATIB: You haven't been so far, why start?

SHADIYAH: I haven't said anything yet.

RATIB: I think the word "rubbish" was used.

SHADIYAH: You can handle this, can't you?

RATIB: Hit me.

SHADIYAH: *(Goes back to leafing through the story)* It feels like—for a while now, your subject matter has become so—limited, and narrow, with all this—navel gazing. That's what I'm trying to say. Your stories have become so—narcissistic. Self-involved. It's like you're disappearing up your own personal asshole and your asshole isn't that interesting. You try to *make* it interesting, but it isn't. And these silly concerns of your characters, and will Cynthia and Nadia admit to their attraction and fall into bed? And will they make room for Hussein? This whole lesbo scene with Hussein joining in *so* reeks of male fantasy, I have to tell you, I was in hysterics.

RATIB: Great.

SHADIYAH: Not laughing with you.

RATIB: It's meant to be amusing.

THE REVIEW

SHADIYAH: Is the intention to be so ludicrous you dismiss the story and begin to wonder about the frustrated sexual life of the writer instead?

(SHADIYAH *and* RATIB *look at each other. He looks like he might respond, but instead:*)

RATIB: Wait a minute. Hold on.

(RATIB *takes a long drink from a glass of water. More from an attempt to suppress what he might say than from any real thirst.*)

SHADIYAH: And what is this long detour about his traumatic toilet training when he was a kid, and how he now can't look down at a toilet bowl without feeling he's staring into the abyss of his life? There's something so—male, and unmanly at the same time. Like you're depicting the worst fetishes of a male psyche, and doing so without much insight.

RATIB: *(Putting the glass down)* Good. Interesting.

SHADIYAH: You know what it is.

RATIB: Good, more.

SHADIYAH: Your stories are now devoid of any real reason to exist. And why do I say that?

RATIB: Why?

SHADIYAH: Okay. And this is actually the crux of what I want to say. There is absolutely no relationship between your stories and the real world anymore. At least the world I thought you lived in. Your stories have almost zero relevancy, no political charge.

RATIB: I'm sorry, I don't mean to sound defensive, but you don't think wading into the gay issue in an Arab context isn't relevant? Or politically charged?

SHADIYAH: Oh please, don't dress up your sexual fantasies in political rhetoric. This is a male fantasy, and if anything reinforces gender stereotypes.

RATIB: Uhm: beg to differ. Nadia and Cynthia become the means by which I get to discuss the Middle-East's disastrous gender relationships, and how desperately they're trying to break out of that.

SHADIYAH: You spend four full pages in a twenty page story detailing girl on girl action. And two of those pages are spent with Nadia's face buried in Cynthia's labia. Where is the politics in that?

RATIB: I think this is where a bit of cultural misunderstanding rears its head. In America, the personal *is* political.

SHADIYAH: In America, everyone disappeared up their personal asshole a long time ago.

RATIB: And I'm sure the Americans would say their personal asshole is political. Otherwise what's the point of politics if it doesn't address what's closest to oneself. In addition, please note that it is Nadia's face buried in Cynthia's...it is the *Arab* woman's face buried between the legs of the American woman. Again, the personal being used to address the patronizing effects of Western feminism, and American liberalism in general. And the final inclusion of Hussein in that bed scene is obviously allegorical and asks the question, "What if everyone got along all at the same time? What would that look like?"

(Slight beat)

SHADIYAH: Ratib. What happened to you?

RATIB: Can I ask if this hostility disguising itself as criticism is actually related to the story? Because it feels extra-textual to me.

SHADIYAH: The first stories I read of yours tackled the world we lived in. I loved that. I loved you because of that. Now when there's even more reason to write about what's happening, you've gone all domestic and petty.

RATIB: For the record, Americans don't appreciate politics in their art. They think they're being preached at, and then you get accused of being didactic.

SHADIYAH: That's preferable to being called irrelevant?

RATIB: I am not irrelevant. I just have to be crafty about how I go about saying what I want to say. It's kind of weirdly like—writing in a politically repressive regime. Except the police state here isn't some baton-wielding goon, but the mind-set that comes down on you if you dare express anything other than petty domestic matters. But what you read is not that. I want them to *think* it is, yes. But that's because I have to plot like a stealth ninja. Cleverly insinuating what I really want to say, without letting on I'm actually saying anything. So they go away thinking I've said nothing. That big central something you think is lacking is actually there, underneath it all. It's me skillfully skirting the political meat of the story while putting it front and center in a completely invisible way. I thought you of all people would pick up on that.

SHADIYAH: Ratib...one of the reasons I wanted to do this face to face is because I wanted to tell you...I don't think it's a good idea for us to continue seeing each other—anymore.

RATIB: *(Slight beat)* You mean we should stop Skyping?

SHADIYAH: No. Well yes. But I mean we should stop seeing each other.

RATIB: So—how would we communicate then? Regular telephone? E-mail?

SHADIYAH: We wouldn't communicate with each other.

RATIB: We're in the middle of planning my trip.

SHADIYAH: I don't think you should come for the summer.

RATIB: When are we going to see each other then?

SHADIYAH: We wouldn't.

(Seeing that RATIB's still not getting it:)

SHADIYAH: Ever again.

RATIB: Wait… Are you breaking up with me?

SHADIYAH: Yes. I appreciate the difference in times zones may be creating a delay in having that sink in.

RATIB: You're breaking up with me?

SHADIYAH: If you step back, and objectively look at our relationship, I think you'll see it's also been missing a big central—something, for a while now. And I don't think that missing part is hiding underneath anything; or stealthily doing its thing. A lot like your recent stories—our relationship has become devoid of any real reason to exist. It's kind of stopped having meaning for me.

RATIB: I knew it…I knew it. This has nothing to do with my story. For all I know you love my story. You're just using my story as a pretext to break up with me. That is low. That is *so* low, hitting me where it hurts just so you can end something. God! That is so below-the-belt; oh my God. —Wait. You're actually breaking up with me?

SHADIYAH: I don't remember you being this—vacuous. For the two years you were studying in Cairo you were engaged, smart; you were curious about people, the government. I'm really serious about this asshole thing: I think you've disappeared up one. Now that you're in the States again, you're slipping back into these non-issues. This garbage of saying nothing at all about things that don't deserve your attention.

RATIB: Not everything has to be political!

SHADIYAH: Yes it does. When your life's on the line, yes it does.

RATIB: Not everyone's life is on the line here!

SHADIYAH: That's why we have to go our separate ways.

RATIB: But what does that have to do with us?

SHADIYAH: I don't have the luxury of compartmentalizing, Ratib. I need a partner. Someone who will go down this road with me, fight with me for the things I believe in.

RATIB: I'll fight with you.

SHADIYAH: No, it's—it won't work.

RATIB: I was there at the rallies, wasn't I?

SHADIYAH: You were there at *one*. And you spent the entire time complaining about the heat, and worrying about communal toilets if you got arrested.

RATIB: That's not a small matter.

SHADIYAH: This summer's going to be a series of planned protests and I need to focus.

RATIB: I'll be there with you.

SHADIYAH: No you won't. Your heart's no where near the front lines of what we're doing here. You're back in la-la land, and maybe that's where you belong.

RATIB: You're such an ideologue, you know that. You're disappearing up something yourself and it's just as dark as any cavity.

SHADIYAH: Goodbye, Ratib.

RATIB: Wait. Wait wait wait. I'm sorry. Don't—. We can't just end it like this. I care for you. I love what you're fighting for. I love your passion. I want to be a part of that. Oh my God, you're seeing someone else.

SHADIYAH: Yes.

RATIB: You are?

SHADIYAH: I've met someone else, yes.

RATIB: I knew it. I knew it! Not my story, not me, it's you. It's been you from the very beginning. This whole review has been a sham. Not me, you! What, I suppose you met him at a rally? Eyes locked over a cloud of tear gas? Rubbed shoulders as the police herded you into a police van? Thrilled at the sound of his sloganeering.
(Mock voice)
"Down with the government", "down with the regime", "democracy now", blah, blah, blah. Is that how it happened? Hands touched as he handed out pamphlets? Did you get all warm inside as you listened to some obvious rhetoric spewing out of his mouth, as he did all he could to get in your pants? Is that it?

SHADIYAH: No. He just writes better stories than you and has more impressive privates. Plus he's not afraid to put his life on the line and doesn't care about communal toilets if he gets arrested.

RATIB: What—a you-know-what—you turned out to be.

SHADIYAH: You've got me. Goodbye, Ratib.

RATIB: And just for the record, my story is *clearly* relevant to the world I live in. You prove it. It certainly captured *you* to a T.
(Counting off on his fingers.)
"Ball-breaker", "cheater", "betrayer", I nailed you. In this country, that's called "portraiture" and craft. Admit it. The story was just too accurate for you to take.

SHADIYAH: There was one good thing about it. It was short. And in that regard, was very reflective of its author's stature. Goodbye. I hope your life rises above the irrelevancy of your art. I mean that sincerely.

(SHADIYAH *switches off. The screen goes blank. Slight beat. Coiled, pissed,* RATIB *also switches off. Slight beat. He picks up the stuffed bear. He looks like he might tear its head off. Instead, if he's gotten up, he sits down again. His face contorts. It's not clear where he's heading with this expression. Then he looks like he might start crying. He clutches the bear to his chest, and puts his head on the table. Then he starts lightly knocking his head against the table as there's a fade to black.)*

END OF PLAY

RADICAL DEPARTURE

RADICAL DEPARTURE was presented by the LIT Council and performed over Zoom in 2021. The cast and creative contributor were:

HASSAN ....Wasim No'mani

Director .... Lori Elizabeth Parquet

CHARACTER

HASSAN, *anywhere from 30s to 40s*

(Airport. GATE AGENT'*s voice is heard.)*

GATE AGENT: *(V O)* This is a pre-boarding announcement for Flight 58 to Seattle. We are inviting passengers with children and those needing special assistance to start boarding at this time. Please have your tickets and IDs ready for inspection. Regular boarding will start shortly.

(Spotlight on HASSAN *as he starts praying the salah in a corner near a departure gate.)*

HASSAN: God forgive me this transgression. Forgive me for using this prayer as a middle finger to all those who are right now eye-balling me. I know I shouldn't be fake praying as a "fuck you" to all those in departure. Who got all shifty in their seats when I started speaking Arabic on the phone. To Mom. In hospital. Giving me all that "Who the fuck are you with your Arabic pointing that loaded language at us right before we board". I can't comfort my mother without you getting all worried? Screw *you* for pointing your loaded fucking eyes at me.

God forgive me for filling my head with expletives in the middle of this prayer. I hope this is more a misdemeanor than a big deal. I know I've done a ton of shit that would give me a front row seat in hell. I know it's "haram", it has to be "haram" using Your name in vain to flip someone off. But it's either this or get in their faces, and God knows where I'd end up if I did that. And forgive me for being such a bad Muslim for never really showing up for prayer. I should be going with my friends to the masjid but instead — well, I don't need to tell *You* what I get up to…pork. Porn. Thinking of bitcoin.

(He looks at someone off-stage.)

Look at that hat-wearing A A R P fool going to the Gate agent and pointing at me. Is this making you crap in your adult diaper, motherfucker?

(Trying to stop himself from getting angry.)

Hassan? …You can't be this angry all the time. Cure me of that please, God. Even as I want to tell that ass-hat with a mustache that looks like pubic hair wandered up to his face and hung over his lip just to tell him what a pussy he is for getting all scared because I'm exercising my right to practice my religion as your forefathers probably did—when they came over and massacred the Natives so they could kneel and pray to their God of *love* and *peace*.

Stop…

I'm going to end up in hospital like moms.

Listen to the words, Hassan, actually listen to the words in the prayer and calm down.

Intention.

Intention.

Pray the prayer. Start again.

(Inhales. Exhales. He raises his hands to his ears.)

"Allahu Akbar."

(He places his right hand over his left hand and looks down.)

"O Allah, how perfect You are and praise be to You. Blessed is Your name, and exalted is Your majesty. There is no god but You. I seek shelter in Allah from the rejected Satan."

(He steals a glance at the offstage people.)

Oh, wow. You are all powerful indeed, Allah, because I just felt a whole new wave of sphincters tighten at the mere mention of Your name. That's power. Oh my God I hate them so much.

(Correcting himself for getting angry)

Hassan!

(He inhales, calms down, prays for real. Though more quietly.)

"Bismillah irrahman irrahim. All praises and thanks be to Allah, the Lord of the worlds, the most Gracious, the most Merciful; Master of the Day of Judgment. You alone do we worship, from You alone do we seek help. Guide us along the straight path. The path of those whom You have favored, not those who have earned Your anger or gone astray."

(More audibly now)

They can't help it….
They've been fed lies. That's all.
They can't think thoughts they've never had.
How would they know with all the crap said about us?
Yes, that's where imagination and empathy should come in.
Where a teeny bit of humanity—imagining other people have it beside yourself, and your own, should kick in. And make you give people you don't know shit about the benefit of the doubt. Is that too much to ask?
It seems yes. It is.
My mom and dad came to a land where Your name, Allah, is repeatedly used as the boogeyman. Why would they come to a place and raise me as a Muslim in a land where Muslims get piñata'd every day? So as to what, give me opportunities? With a side order of shame; and being pissed off all the time? And always having to explain myself? And then explain some more

when my clear explanations clearly enunciated in a civil and polite manner are met with dead eyes? I could be in the embrace of this very prayer I'm trying to pray but instead I'm ready to kneecap someone. No.
This…
this is going to eat me up and spit me out in little pieces.
We can't all be in our corners staring daggers and spitting bullets. That's the cliff edge. Over and out. Circular firing squad. What's that verse? "O mankind, indeed We have made you different peoples and tribes so that you may get to know one another"?

So get to know them, for fuck's sake (sorry, sorry for the expletives).
We're supposed to be different to each other.
That's the way You made us, right?
If we were all one big indistinguishable amoeba, what would be the point of anything? We'd be one big blob of—what?
We have to try and get to know one another, if we want to make it and survive. And since we're all basically strangers to each other, we have to…
we've no choice but to lean in to each other.
And when we do lean into each other…
we lean into You, right?

Forgive me my puny thoughts in the very midst of the sacredness I'm supposed to surrender to. But you want us to think things through, don't You? Trying to understand the very people I want to scream at *is* the struggle. Bridging that gulf *is* the prayer. And that's supposed to open me up to You. Right?

Okay.

Okay.

Good can come of this.
This is good.

I'm feeling the feels, God.
I want to surrender my anger. I want to hand it over for the concealed firearm it is. I don't want it on me. I don't want to be scared of people who are scared of me. I don't want to wish them horrible deaths. I'm going to go over to that guy and introduce myself. I will smile. I will break the ice with a simple "hello". And then I'll follow that with a, "Hey, I couldn't help notice the way you reacted when I started speaking Arabic. And I know my praying might seem threatening, strange to say, but my mother is in hospital, you see. She's about to have heart surgery. I wanted to comfort her in the language she knows best. We were actually speaking that silly love language that families have when they want to cheer each other up. You know the kind. It was really a combo of Arabic and nonsense words. You know—the silly nicknames, and the 'coochy-coos', and—that kind of silly stuff. I'm sorry if my speaking Arabic scared you. I totally understand given the years of hearing crap about all things—well—Arab, and Muslim. And when I started praying: I get it. But honestly—I got angry at you and the others for giving me nasty looks. And I thought—

if they want fear—I'll give it to them.

I'll serve it up on a—well, on a prayer rug and make them lose their shit. Childish, I know. But:

The real real reason I started praying was—because…

I'm scared my mother might not make it.

And I got angry that right when I'm feeling this scared, and moms is also terrified but trying not to show it, because she doesn't want her son to lose it over the phone, because then *she'll* lose it, and we'll both embarrass each other with just this…terror we're both feeling. Because she doesn't know, and *I* don't know if I'll get there before the operation and maybe not see her again. That's what we're both thinking.

And then she starts talking about what's in the freezer for me to eat when I get in. She'd made my favorite dish, `bamya', which is like this meat and okra stew, though you can also make it without meat if you're a vegetarian; and if you get warm pita bread you can scoop it up and it's really yummy.

That's what she wanted to tell me. Because talking about food meant we didn't have to talk about the other thing we didn't want to talk about. That I might not see her again.

So you see,
when I noticed you all giving me funny looks, and I understood what those looks were, I—reacted. By praying. Because I knew you'd start flipping out. Which I know God must just be loving, using Him to flip someone off.
And the sad thing is I was so pissed off...
I never even got around to praying for my mom.

So I'm sorry.
And if you'll allow me...
I'd like to hug you now."
Yeah?
Yeah.
I think I'll say all that.
He might even hug me back.
Why not. It could happen.
Good.
Good.
And I'll hug anyone else who wants to be hugged. So much love could happen right here in this departure lounge. We could turn this into a love fest. Your Will be done. "Bismillah irrahman irrahim": "The Merciful, the Compassionate". Your attributes made manifest

right here and now. The power of prayer indeed. If that's not being a good Muslim….

Thank you. Thank you God for leading me out of this dark little hole I was digging for myself.
Alright.
Yes. Yes. I'll finish up the prayer and then go over to him and…

(He looks at another area off-stage. Slight beat as he realizes what's happening.)

He called the cops.
They called the cops on me.
I don't believe it.
They called the goddamn fucking cops on me. Jesus fucking Christ.
Well fuck you all too.

(For a moment, he's locked back in that anger. Then, perhaps, he closes his eyes. He takes a deep breath. Opens his eyes again. Blackout)

END OF PLAY

www.ingramcontent.com/pod-product-compliance
Lightning Source LLC
Chambersburg PA
CBHW061759110426
42742CB00012BB/2188